NOT MY WILL
BUT THINE

COMING TO TERMS WITH
THINGS YOU CAN'T CHANGE

BRENDA POINSETT

BROADMAN
&HOLMAN
PUBLISHERS

Nashville, Tennessee

0-8054-6369-0

Published by Broadman & Holman Publishers, Nashville, Tennessee
Page Composition: Desktop Miracles, Dallas, Texas
Acquisitions and Development Editor: Vicki Crumpton

Dewey Decimal Classification: 248.8
Subject Heading: PRAYER—CHRISTIANITY
Library of Congress Card Catalog number: 97-50135

Unless otherwise stated, all Scripture citation is from the King James Version. Other versions cited are NASB, the New American Standard Bible, © the Lockman Foundation, 1960, 1962, 1963, 1968, 1971, 1972, 1973, 1975, 1977, used by permission; NIV, the Holy Bible, New International Version, copyright © 1973, 1978, 1984 by International Bible Society; RSV, Revised Standard Version of the Bible, copyrighted 1946, 1952, © 1971, 1973; Phillips, reprinted with permission of Macmillan Publishing Co., Inc. from J. B. Phillips: The New Testament in Modern English, revised edition, © J. B. Phillips 1958, 1960, 1972; TLB, The Living Bible, copyright © Tyndale House Publishers, Wheaton, Ill., 1971, used by permission; the Holy Bible, New Century Version, © 1987, 1988, 1991 by Word Publishing, Dallas, Texas 75039, used by permission; NLT, the New Life Testament, The New Testament in the Language of the People, by Charles B. Williams, copyright © 1937, 1966, 1986, by Holman Bible Publishers, used by permission; and The Good News Bible, the Bible in Today's English Version; Old Testament: copyright © American Bible Society 1976; New Testament: copyright © American Bible Society 1966, 1971, 1976, used by permission.

Library of Congress Cataloging-in-Publication Data
Poinsett, Brenda.
    Not my will but thine: coming to terms with things you can't change / Brenda Poinsett
      p.   cm.
    Includes bibliographical references.
    ISBN 0-8054-6369-0
    1. Prayer—Christianity.   2. Resignation.   I. Title
BV227.P65   1998
248.8'6—dc21
                          97-50135
                            CIP

1 2 3 4 5 02 01 00 99 98

NOT MY WILL
BUT THINE

To Peggy
who knows how to pray in light of the cross

CONTENTS

CONTENTS

CONTENTS

ACKNOWLEDGMENTS

Even if I wanted to, I couldn't write a book alone. I need input from others—their prayers, encouraging words, resources, and examples. A book is stronger and richer when it is a group project.

Input: I'm grateful for the insight and criticisms offered by Virginia Muir, LaVonne Neff, Sam and Sandy Carnell, Dennis and Kay Whitaker, and Vicki Crumpton, acquisitions and development editor at Broadman and Holman Publishers. Dennis deserves special recognition because he persevered in critiquing the entire manuscript while he had deadlines to meet.

Prayers: What would a book on prayer be without prayer support? I appreciate the prayers of Marge Braden, Peggy Brooks, Donna Williams, fellow church members at Limestone Baptist Church, and various friends at Bedford's Free Methodist Church such as Susan Miller and Sandy Carnell. They prayed for me at various stages of the book's development.

Encouraging Words: Mary Maynard, of Bedford Bible Bookstore, and Jerry Hughes, librarian at Oakland City University's Bedford campus, have that special sensitivity of knowing how and when to encourage a writer.

Resources: Thanks again to Jerry at OCU-B's library, and thanks to the librarians at Bedford Public Library and to Catherine Schulze at Roberts Library of Southwestern Seminary, Fort Worth, Texas. Whatever resources I asked for, they found for me.

Examples: Many thanks to those who were willing to let me use their personal experiences as illustrations. This includes Peggy Brooks, Russ Weiss, Allan Poage, and others. Most preferred to remain anonymous so their names and circumstances have been altered to protect their privacy.

This thanks also includes the many people whose experiences had already appeared in print and who graciously gave me permission to reuse their words.

Special thanks goes to two men: my husband, Bob Poinsett, and my teaching colleague, Paul Zell. Bob's help includes all of these categories—input, prayers, encouraging words, resources, and examples. We walked the road together that led to my discovering how to pray in light of the cross. I'm glad he was there for that journey and for the journey of writing this book.

Paul taught my classes for me so I could focus on writing. Neither of us knew when he agreed to do this that before the semester was over, Paul too would be walking the way of the cross. The brightness of the integrity of his faith during this time inspired me during the final days of bringing this book to completion. Those days were also Paul's final days—at least on this earth. So for now I want his family to know of my gratitude. The day will come, though, when I will get to thank Paul face to face.

PART I

THE DILEMMA

Struggling with What We Can't Change

"Father, if thou be willing, remove this cup from me: nevertheless not my will, but thine, be done."

LUKE 22:42

CHAPTER 1

IN THE JAWS OF A VISE

*It is not part of the Christian hope to look for a life
in which a man is saved from all trouble and
distress; the Christian hope is that a man in Christ
can endure any kind of trouble and distress, and
remain erect all through them, and come out to
glory on the other side.*[1]

WILLIAM BARCLAY

When Russ gave sixteen-year-old Sara permission to
cruise around town with her friends, he didn't dream that
three hours later, she would look ". . . as though she had
been placed in a meat grinder and broken to pieces."[2]

On an unfamiliar road, the driver of the car Sara was in
ran a stop sign and hit two trees. Sara suffered massive and
deep cuts all over her body. Her teeth and gums were visible through the gaping cuts to her jaws, neck, and face. Her
left lung had collapsed; her pelvis was broken. She had
deep lacerations to her arms and legs with tissue protrud-
ing from the cuts. Russ said, "I just stood and looked at my
daughter in disbelief. . . . There was nothing I could do."[3]

***

Peggy's fingers were often infected, and the infection didn't readily respond to treatment. To find out why the infection kept recurring, Peggy underwent many medical tests. The resulting diagnosis: scleroderma.

Peggy had never heard of scleroderma before. When her doctor explained it to her, he said, "Scleroderma is not a fatal disease. You will be able to handle all the symptoms as they come up. What you will mostly be aware of is not getting any wrinkles as you age."[4]

Peggy thought, "Gee, I can handle this!"[5]

The doctor suggested she write the Scleroderma Foundation for more information. From the information she received, Peggy discovered she was facing an ugly, disabling, and eventually fatal disease.[6] There was no known cure.

***

Mark had a passion for books; his enthusiasm made him a successful area sales representative for a major book publisher. The publisher, though, took a number of risky ventures; the company lost money. To recover, sales were turned over to an outside agency, and all the sales representatives were fired. Mark cleaned out his desk, drove home, and went to bed. He stayed there for days before he told his wife he had been fired.

***

Barbara noticed that many of those in her Christian student group had trouble conversing with and being comfortable around non-Christians. Barbara didn't; she moved easily among Christians and non-Christians. She never actually compromised her beliefs, but she was often coy in what she revealed and didn't reveal. She saw herself as savvy and sophisticated because she successfully moved in and out of both groups.

At the Christian student group's fall retreat, Barbara was unexpectedly challenged by the emphasis on holy living. Her heart stirred the way it had some nine years earlier when she became a Christian. Realizing that God was speaking to her, she thought, *Oh, God, please don't ask me to change. I can't handle being different.*

***

Greg had a goal that he carried within himself; he knew that some day he was going to be a professional baseball player. This goal was nurtured by his friends and coaches who told him how good he was and by his father who often said, "Son, you can be anything you want to be."

After college, when he tried out for the pros, he was accepted by a farm club. Greg wasn't discouraged by this; he was a hard worker and saw this as a rung on the ladder to success. He was stunned when the manager called him in at the end of his first season and said, "Greg, I'm going to level with you. You don't have what it takes to make it in professional baseball. I advise you to start planning another career."

***

When Tom, the church's youth director, asked for adults under forty to chaperone the youth attending the state convention, forty-five-year-old Jill couldn't believe her ears. While she didn't work with the youth on a regular basis, she always volunteered to chaperone their out-of-town trips. She thought, *And now because of my age, I'm not capable any longer?* She couldn't stop thinking about it during the morning's sermon. She hated the thought of growing old and was going to fight it with all the resources she had.

After church, Tom saw Jill in the foyer. He asked, "Can I count on you to chaperone the youth convention?" Startled, she just looked at him. Then she realized, *He doesn't know how old I am. Oh, good!* "Why sure, Tom, I'll be glad to help you out."

***

Allan and Ruth were having one of those end-of-the-day, leisurely kind of conversations that only people who have been married a long time can have. They talked about things that mattered and also inconsequential things, often blending one with the other. Sometimes there were comfortable pauses of silence, as each dealt with his or her own thoughts. Then one of them would pick up the conversation again. It was their way of unwinding before they fell asleep. During an unusually long period of silence, Allan heard some strange gurgling sounds from Ruth's side of the bed. Allan said, "What is it, Ruth?" There was no answer. "Ruth, Ruth?" Allan turned on the light and saw this strange look on Ruth's face. He touched her and she didn't respond. He called 911. The emergency personnel came and rushed Ruth to the hospital where the attending physician pronounced her dead from an aneurysm.

At first glance, these stories may seem unrelated, but they aren't. Sooner or later, we all come up against something we can't change.

* *Accidents.* It may be something that comes as starkly and abruptly as Sara's accident, a natural disaster, or a violent act of crime. After the fact, these events cannot be changed.

* *Terminal illness.* The future may seem like something that can't be changed for those like Peggy who have a terminal or incurable illness. Some people might want to argue with this label and say, "Miracles are always possible," but for many the miracles will not come.

* *Job termination.* A person fired from his job may be able to change his future, but he can't change his past. He

may want to push the replay button on the recorder of life, but he will discover the replay button doesn't work. The tape of life cannot be rewound.

* *God's will*. While we may be wrong in how we interpret God's will, the kind of life he wants us to live will not change. If we want to be God's obedient children, then we will do what he wants.

* *Personal limitations*. The self-help books we devour, the seminars we attend, the magazines we read, the educational and motivational videos we watch imply we can change our looks, our weight, our mood, our self-esteem, and our income. Like Greg's father told him, they tell us, "You can be anything you want to be!" But all of us can't; there's a limit to what we can change about ourselves.

* *Aging*. That Jill was discouraged by Tom's age-specific request is understandable; nevertheless, she will have to come to grips some time with the aging process. Face-lifts, hair-dying, and weight-watching may camouflage the aging process. Exercise, nutrition, and hormone-replacement may slow it down, but aging is inevitable.

* *Death*. America's baby boomers who are turning fifty have challenged every stage of their lives. Many of them believe they can live forever, if only they eat right and get their 10K runs every morning. The best nutrition and exercise program available may add two to seven years to life, but it will not change the fact of Hebrews 9:27: "And as it is appointed unto men once to die."

Some people may be reluctant to think in terms of what they can't change. They are optimists who see themselves in control of their destiny. They thrive on self-help material that continually assures them change is possible.

Christians especially may bristle at the idea of something being unchangeable. After all, we have the best self-help material available—the Bible. We are resurrection people; we are eternal optimists. One of our frequently quoted slogans is "Prayer changes things."

I'm addicted to self-help materials and to the power of prayer. I believe in the possibility of change; yet, as the examples of Russ, Peggy, Mark, Barbara, Jill, Greg, and Allan illustrate, we do come up against things we can't change.

When I started encountering things I couldn't change, I found a void in the self-help materials and I found my way of praying ineffective. I needed help in coping with what I could not change.

TRAPPED IN A VISE

Coping with unchangeables involves struggle, more intense for some than for others. The struggle may involve feelings such as fragility, agitation, anxiety, insecurity, discouragement, fear, anger, despair, resentment, and grief. Left unresolved, these powerful emotions rob us of our peace of mind. Left unexpressed, they can cause us to become cynical about life or hopeless about the future.

Coping with what we can't change requires adjustment. Evaluation and restructuring may be in order. Choices will need to be made. Relationships may be affected, especially our relationship with God. We may feel like he abandoned us or betrayed us. We may decide God is untrustworthy, or we may feel like it is futile to continue to try to please him.

Coming up against things we can't change is like being in the jaws of a vise. As a child I liked to rummage around in my grandfather's messy workshop. One of the items that fascinated me was the vise. I picked up blocks of wood that were scattered on the floor and put them in the vise. I turned the crank until the block or blocks were tightly in place, sometimes squeezing extra hard. I tried various blocks, sometimes a combination of two. I was fascinated with how the vise held the blocks securely in place, and I was fascinated by the power I had over the blocks. I was in control.

When we come up against something we can't change, we aren't in control. As the jaws of the vise move in on us, we struggle and push against them. The vise squeezes us into a position we don't want to be in. We can push and push, but these jaws won't budge. We want to escape, but we can't. How then do we live with what we can't change?

A SOLUTION

What we can't change is such a broad category that research doesn't show one solution that works for every person, which is just as well. If we had a research-based, foolproof solution, we might become glib about people's struggles. Coping with what we can't change involves grappling with the harsh realities of life. To pin a snappy, three-point, works-every-time formula on that kind of struggle is to trivialize it. It minimizes a person's pain and ignores individual circumstances.

Coping strategies vary. Some are effective; others are ineffective. Some are healthy; others are unhealthy. Some people cope by denying there is a dilemma. Others count on time as the solution—over time, they assure themselves, they will forget about what they can't change. Some people withdraw. They don't want to have anything to do with others, and sometimes they don't want to have anything to do with God. Some try distracting themselves through activities; others try positive thinking. Some count on the counsel of friends, support groups, or psychotherapists. Others try to comfort themselves through legal prescription drugs or through illegal drugs or alcohol.

Some people seem to adjust readily to what they can't change, while others become weighed down by the struggle. Some become stuck—unwilling or unable to move forward into the future. They need someone whose hand they can hold and whose leadership they can trust to pull them out of the slough of despondency and help them regain the joy of living.

The person who helps can't be just anybody. It has to be someone who has struggled with something he couldn't change. Those of us trying to cope with what we can't change can relate best to someone who has also experienced the jaws of the vise and pushed against them.

The premise of this book is that Jesus is just such a person. It may be hard for some of us to believe that Jesus—God incarnate—struggled with something he couldn't change. Jesus had the power of heaven at his disposal. He came to earth to initiate change and succeeded. He was an agent of change on many occasions; and yet there was one thing he couldn't change—Jesus couldn't change his destiny to die on the cross.

Jesus was to be the suffering Messiah. His dying on the cross was a voluntary act, but in another sense, it wasn't. If he wanted to be the obedient Son, there was only one way before him—the way of the cross.

From where we stand, Jesus' triumph was so certain that it looks like it was effortless and without strain. His courage was so calm, so sure, so seemingly inevitable, that it almost looks automatic. But if we move closer to him, if we walk with him from his baptism to the cross, focusing on his prayer life, we will see that it wasn't automatic. He, too, struggled with what he could not change; therefore, we can relate to him and trust his leadership.

WALKING WITH JESUS

Jesus said, "He that followeth me shall not walk in darkness, but shall have the light of life" (John 8:12b). When we walk with Jesus, he will light up our path. He will help us see more clearly what we are up against. He will help us see possibilities that we didn't even know existed. He will show us how we can cope with what we can't change.

If we want "the light of life," we must take the whole walk from Jesus' baptism to his death on the cross. If we look at just one prayer Jesus prayed, we might not get the complete picture of what is involved in coping with what we can't change. We need the broad picture to understand the nature of our struggle.

Eventually as we walk with Jesus, we will begin to identify with him. A kinship will develop so we will be able to say along with him, "Now is my soul troubled" (John 12:27a). This kinship ignites hope—if Jesus struggled and endured, perhaps I can too.

Identification leads to imitation. We may see patterns in the way that he prayed—patterns that may provide the breakthrough we need to give us the peace we long for or restore the joy we lost. We may hear the words he used in prayer and make those words our words so they give voice to our agony and bring relief. We may note where he prayed and find new places to offer our own prayers. We may be surprised and yet relieved by his honesty; this may encourage us to express honestly our emotions to God. We may marvel at his gratitude during both good times and bad times and wonder if gratitude could play a part in re-solving our own situation. When we pray as Jesus prayed, we will gain specific ways for coping with what we can't change.

Intimacy results when we walk with a person sharing his life experiences, when we hear his prayers, when we see things from his perspective, and when we hear his cries of anguish. In the "fellowship of his sufferings" we can *know* Jesus (Phil. 3:10) and find strength to live with what we cannot change.

MAKING YOUR WILL MINE

How have I been trying to cope with what I can't change?

What will I gain by praying Jesus' way?

How are identification, imitation, and intimacy related?

"O Light that followest all my way,
I yield my flick-'ring torch to thee."[7]

CHAPTER 2

FINDING THE RIGHT LABEL

We can expect his [God's] dealings with us to be
unique. They will have a certain "ring" to them
that is unlike any other experience we have ever
had, yet somehow we will know, as Isaiah did,
that this is God, the Holy One, revealing himself in
his own way.[1]

JOHN CLAYPOOL

Before beginning our walk with Jesus, we need to ask, When is something unchangeable and when is it not? In a book that focuses on what we can't change, we wouldn't want to encourage anyone to call something unchangeable when it is. For good mental and spiritual health, none of us should be quick to label something unchangeable.

DETERMINING THE POSSIBILITY OF CHANGE

All of us need to see possibilities for change when they exist. Possibilities propel us forward, keeping us optimistic

13

and hopeful. They enable us to believe we have some control over our lives. When we see ourselves as having no control, life is miserable.

The Bible teaches us to expect change. Jesus taught and encouraged us to believe all kinds of things are possible (Matt. 21:22; Mark 9:23; Mark 11:22–24; Luke 17:6). To call something unchangeable too quickly is to close the door on faith-stretching experiences where miracles may occur. The possibility of change makes the Christian life exciting and dynamic.

WHAT'S CHANGEABLE

With some things, it is easy to apply the "changeable" label. We can readily recognize when earnest prayer would help us make changes:

* "God, help me to manage my time so I can cover my workload and still have time for my family."
* "Father, I'm lonely. Help me to have the courage to make friends."
* "Lord, help me find a way to break the tension between Jan and me. I don't want my relationship with her to be this way."

While the solutions may not be simple or come easily in each of these cases, the possibility for change is obvious.

WHAT'S NOT CHANGEABLE

With some things, it's readily and painfully obvious we can't change them:

* After an automobile accident, we cannot go back and reduce our speed or take another route no

matter how much we might fantasize about doing so.

* After a tornado destroys our home, we cannot go back to the way things were.
* After we lose a family member in death, we cannot bring that person back to life. The finality of death is hard to accept.

WHAT'S HARD TO LABEL

In between what we can readily identify as changeable and what's obviously unchangeable are hard-to-label items. Divorce is an example. In many states it only takes one person wanting to get a divorce to get one. Does the non-consenting spouse pray for God to restore the marriage, or does he or she ask God's help with adjusting to being single?

In *Hope Has Its Reasons,* Rebecca Manley Pippert tells the true story of a minister whose wife wanted out of the marriage. She said to her husband, "The marriage is not what I want, and I don't feel any love for you. I want out. I'm filing for a divorce."[2]

The minister had not seen it coming. Devastated and shocked, he said to his wife, "Please, don't do this. Let's try to make this work. Please don't get a divorce."[3]

The wife agreed not to file right away, but she did not stay with him. The minister began praying for his wife regularly. He told Pippert, "I began to love her in a way I had never known. . . . It was through prayer that I found the resources to love and forgive her."[4]

Unbeknownst to his wife, he often walked around her apartment at night and prayed for her, asking God to bless her. He saw his wife occasionally, but she held out no hope that they would reunite. Yet he believed that if he were constant and faithful, she would change her mind and return.

One day she came to him and said, "I have given up a lot of things I used to believe in. But I can't let go of my faith in Jesus because I've seen him so clearly in you. . . . But I haven't changed my mind about marriage, and I have decided to file for divorce now."[5]

Following the divorce, the members of his church urged him to find a woman to share his life with. Like the Old Testament prophet Hosea who followed God's instructions to love the wife who left him, this minister remained faithful and prayed daily for his wife.

Ten years after his wife left him, she came back, and they were reunited in marriage.

I marvel at this story, yet I'm reluctant to say to my friends who are unwillingly facing a divorce, "Hang in there. Keep praying and you will get your mate back." Even the minister acknowledged that this approach wouldn't necessarily be God's calling to everyone.[6]

How does a person know whether to persevere in hoping a broken marriage will be mended or to accept it as over and move on with establishing a new life as a single person? How does someone like Peggy, diagnosed with scleroderma, know whether to accept the diagnosis and live with it or to believe in God for a miracle cure? Should Greg, who thought he was destined to be a professional baseball player, accept the advice of his manager to quit, or should he continue to try? How does a person know when to accept self-limitations and when to keep pursuing dreams?

In situations like these, knowing if something is changeable or unchangeable is difficult to evaluate. We want to hope for the best; we don't want to surrender too soon where there is still hope for change. We want to be faith-believing Christians who expect miracles. On the other hand, continually anticipating change might keep us from receiving the serenity and strength that comes with acceptance. It might keep us from making the necessary adjustments that would create new lives for ourselves.

Finding the label that applies is not easy. We may spend a lot of time thinking about it, vacillating about the label. One day when our hopes are high, we call our situation changeable. A few days later, after some discouraging remarks from others or a stressful day, we may label it unchangeable. We may talk with friends, our pastor, or even a professional counselor, trying to find the definitive label.

What we seek is an inner moment when we know without a doubt what the label is. The moment may come because we decide, *This is what I can live with. I have to make a decision.* It may come because it seems like the logical thing to do. Or, it may come for us in prayer—as it did for Jesus after a long period of reflection, inner struggle, and deepening insight.

JESUS' SITUATION

Exactly when Jesus' consciousness of his earthly role began, we don't know. Surely he did not know it when he was a baby in the manger or as a small child. I can't imagine a three-year-old knowing he was the Son of God who would someday die on a cross for the salvation of men and women.

WHEN DID JESUS KNOW?

At some time in his youth, Jesus must have consciously discovered his unique relationship to God. Maybe it began with his first visit to the temple in Jerusalem when he was twelve (Luke 2:41–50). Jesus was left behind by his parents when they started back to their home in Nazareth. When they discovered Jesus wasn't with them, Joseph and Mary went back to Jerusalem to look for him. "After three days they found him in the temple courts, sitting among the teachers, listening to them and asking them questions. . . . When his parents saw him, they were astonished. His mother said to him, 'Son, why have you treated us like this? Your father and I have been anxiously searching for you.'

" 'Why were you searching for me?' he asked. 'Didn't you know I had to be in my Father's house?' " (Luke 2:46–49, NIV).

In his *Commentary on Luke,* Ray Summers writes, "The question was literally, 'You were aware, were you not, that I must be in the things (or, in the places) of my Father?' "[7] " 'In my Father's places' would refer to the Temple buildings; this was God's house; he was God's Son; he belonged here."[8] Jesus' words indicate he had some understanding of his unique relationship with God, yet he went back to Nazareth as a boy, obedient to his parents (Luke 2:51).

We don't know what happened in Jesus' life in the next eighteen years other than he worked as a carpenter. While he worked, perhaps he pondered what his unique relationship with God the Father meant. What kind of work did God have for him to do? Would God want him to speak to people? How would he speak? Scathing like the prophets of old? Or gentle and understanding? How would people receive his message? Would he have to leave Nazareth? Would he face danger?

Some readers may be uncomfortable with the idea that Jesus would have asked these kinds of questions, and yet asking them is a normal part of maturing. If Jesus fully entered the human situation, then he had to grow into a consciousness of who he was, and he had to discover his mission. Luke said, "Jesus increased in wisdom and stature, and in favor with God and man" (2:52), and the writer of Hebrews said Jesus "learned through his sufferings to be obedient" (5:8, TEV) and "was made perfect" to become "the source of eternal salvation" (5:9, TEV).

THE DEFINING MOMENT

Jesus needed a moment when the questions would end, and he would know the direction of his future. What or who would be the catalyst for bringing his questions to an end?

Elton Trueblood writes that John the Baptist was the instrument of arousing.[9] Trueblood states, "John went throughout the whole territory of the Jordan River preaching, 'Turn away from your sins' " (Luke 3:3, TEV). Like the prophets of old, John confronted the people with their sins. When they repented, John baptized them. John's preaching "struck the moral nerve" of the people[10] and they flocked out to hear him. Jesus left Nazareth and joined those flocking to the Jordan (Matt. 3:13).

Jesus asked John to baptize him. As Jesus was being baptized, he prayed (Luke 3:21). Heaven opened, indicating that a revelation from God would follow.[11] The Holy Spirit descended on Jesus "in bodily form like a dove" (Luke 3:22, NIV), and a voice from heaven said, "Thou art my beloved Son; in thee I am well pleased" (Luke 3:22).

God's words were very significant. What he said was composed of two texts from the Old Testament. The texts were very familiar to Jews and would, therefore, have been familiar to Jesus.

"Thou art my Son" is from Psalm 2:7. This messianic psalm foretold "the triumph of the Messiah, the anointed King of God. So, then, when Jesus heard this voice, he knew himself to be the Messiah, the King sent by God."[12]

"In whom my soul delights" [I am well pleased] is from Isaiah's description of the servant of the Lord (Isa. 42:1b, RSV). The portrait culminates in the sufferings of one who was wounded for our transgressions and bruised for our iniquities, the one on whom the chastisement of our peace fell, the one who was to be like a sheep dumb before its shearers (Isa. 53).

"So when Jesus heard the voice, he knew that he was God's chosen Messiah, but he also knew that the way for him was the way of the Cross."[13] His future was defined.

LEARNING FROM JESUS

What can we learn from Jesus' defining moment that will help us in finding the right label—changeable or unchangeable—for our situation?

1. *Jesus prayed.* While some would consider it an overstatement, Elton Trueblood refers to Jesus' need to have his future defined as a crisis experience. He writes, "The crisis was so great that prayer was the only appropriate response."[14] After his many hours of contemplation at Nazareth, Jesus needed to hear from God.

Couldn't God have simply supplied the power and direction Jesus needed without his having to ask? Why did Jesus need to pray? To answer that, we need to remember why we all need to ask. Our asking opens our wills to God, giving him the channel he needs to respond. Asking indicates a willingness to receive.

Jesus was made like us; therefore, he needed to open his will to God just as any of us do in order to let God respond to us and work through us. To suppose that Jesus' divineness freed him from operating under the limitations that we do is to undermine the truth of John 1:14: "And the Word [mind of God] was made flesh, and dwelt among us."

As important as prayer was to Jesus' defining moment, we must be careful not to conclude, "If we just pray, then we will know if something is unchangeable or not." That would be an oversimplification of Jesus' experience. Other dynamics were involved.

2. *Jesus put himself in a place to hear from God.* Jesus, who was without sin, didn't *need* to be baptized, yet he left his home in Nazareth to go to Judea to identify himself with a revival movement. Jesus was ready to fulfill all righteousness (Matt. 3:15), so he put himself in a place where God was working.

If we want to discover what we can change and what we can't, we may need to move ourselves to a place where we can hear from God. The Bible says, "Draw nigh to God, and he will draw nigh to you" (James 4:8a). The place in which we "draw nigh" can be an actual physical location or it can be a place of attitude.

After months of sleepless nights, stewing and brewing over his lost job, Mark was persuaded to go on a retreat. At first his emotions and spirit felt sealed off. He thought, *This is a waste of time. I should be home working on job applications so I can return to book selling.* Mark liked to sing, so he joined in with the others. Then the retreat leader called on him to pray. Little by little through the retreat activities, Mark unzipped his heart. Thirty-six hours later, when he was praying under a tree by the lake, Mark heard God speak, "Mark, I want you to embark on a new adventure. I have a new career in mind for you." Mark left the retreat relieved. On Monday he enrolled in his local community college to prepare for a new career.

Instead of moving ourselves to a physical place like a retreat site, we may have to move ourselves to a place of attitude. We may have to bring ourselves to a willingness to hear what God has to say. The first place—the physical place—is easier to reach than the second. It may take us a while to get to the attitude place. Before we arrive, we may have to ask ourselves, Do we really want a label on what we are trying to define? Do we really want to know if something is unchangeable or not?

3. *Jesus knew the Scriptures.* Recognizing God's answer to our prayer for the right label is not as simple as recognizing God's answer to a request for something tangible. When we pray for three new members for our Bible study group, we know the prayer is answered when we have three new members. When we pray for money to repair our car, we know the prayer is answered when the money is in hand. When we pray for a label for our situation, the answer will be intangible. In our inner space, where we can't touch it, God's answer will come.

However, other voices also reside in our inner space. They want to answer us—cultural voices, the comments of family members and friends, and our own desires and wishes. How do we recognize God's voice from among the others?

At Jesus' baptism, he recognized God's answer because he knew the Scriptures and he knew their meaning. The words God spoke, "Thou art my beloved Son; in thee I am well pleased" (Luke 3:22b), are beautiful words—words that would be welcomed by a child on any occasion, but they had special significance for Jesus because he knew the Scriptures and knew what they meant.

Noticing this about Jesus is not to imply that God always answers with specific words and phrases from the Bible, but it does remind us that God always answers in line with his character as revealed in the Bible. God's answer to us will have a biblical precedent. We can test an inner voice by asking, *Does this sound like something God would say?*

Not knowing what the Bible says should never keep us from praying, but if we are earnest about wanting God's label, we will study the Bible as well as pray. Prayer should not be an isolated area of our lives. It should be interwoven in the fabric of our lives right along with Bible study and other spiritual disciplines. Knowing what the Bible says will enhance our praying and improve our ability to recognize God's answers.

As we continue our walk with Jesus, we'll see these three lessons from Jesus' first recorded prayer reinforced. We'll learn more about Jesus putting himself in places to hear from God, about how he prayed, and about how he used the Scriptures. In the meantime, practicing these three principles will enable us to learn God's label for our situation. His label is something we don't want to miss.

WHY DO WE WANT GOD'S LABEL?

When we know and accept God's label for our situation, the inner vacillating ends. Our future direction will become clearer. We'll know whether to pursue change or whether to accept the unchangeable. Either direction will not necessarily be easy, but we will have the inner certainty and confidence that comes when we know we are doing God's will.

We will also receive God's power. While Jesus prayed at his baptism, the Holy Spirit came down upon him in bodily form like a dove. Herbert Lockyer said Jesus could not have commenced his ministry without the gift of the Holy Spirit.[15] He needed power for his mission.

We need God's power when we are trying to make changes or when we are trying to live with what we can't change. The minister in Pippert's story said, "It was through prayer that I found the resources to love and forgive her [his wife]."[16] God said to him, "I will give you the strength you need day by day, moment by moment."[17] God wants to give us his power (Luke 11:13), and he will when we seek his label.

MAKING YOUR WILL MINE

What dilemma am I currently facing?

How am I labeling it? How are others labeling it?
__ changeable
__ unchangeable
__ uncertain

Where can I go to discover God's label?

I will move to a place to hear from God by:
__ opening my will to receive God's help.
__ studying the Bible to improve my ability to recognize God's answer.

"God, grant me the serenity
To accept the things I cannot change;
Courage to change the things I can;
And the wisdom to know the difference."[18]

CHAPTER 3

DID JESUS NEED TO PRAY?

*If Christ had not felt the need to pray, He might
seem to us, especially in the light of His sinlessness,
an impressive and awesome figure, but He would
not seem close to our common lives. We need to
pray, and He means more to us because He, too,
needed to pray.*[1]

ELTON TRUEBLOOD

Lois sat in Sue's living room and poured out her frustration. She said, "I can't concentrate any more. What am I going to do? I'm afraid I'm going to lose my job."

Tears began to flow as Lois described how she could no longer keep up with her coworkers. Occasionally she got up and paced the floor and then returned to the couch. Frightened and anxious, Lois said to Sue, "What's wrong with me?"

Sue took hold of both of Lois' hands, looked directly in her eyes, and gently but firmly said, "Your husband died; you must accept it and move on."

That was exactly what Lois needed to do, but she bristled at Sue's suggestion. Sue made it sound so easy, as if there was nothing to it; no struggle involved.

Some of us have a similar view of what Jesus had to do. As one of my college students wrote in a paper, "Many people thought how much of a rebel Jesus was. The way I see it, he was simply doing the work of His Father, God. Jesus was labeled as a sinner because He healed many people on the Sabbath, but again, I believe He was just doing work for God. This was planned and meant to be according to God's word."

JESUS' TENSION AND TEMPTATIONS

When God's voice spoke to Jesus at his baptism, Jesus learned what was before him. He received his life's direction—a direction that involved suffering and the cross. At the same time Jesus was empowered for the task, so it was just a simple matter of doing what God wanted, right?

No, it wasn't a simple matter.

THE IMMEDIATE STRUGGLE

After Jesus' baptism, the Spirit drove Jesus out into the wilderness (Mark 1:12) where he fasted (Luke 4:2). To the Jews, fasting was a means by which strong emotions could be expressed. Fasting was connected with mourning and urgent supplication. At this time of heightened emotion and sensitivity for Jesus, Satan tempted him three times.

1. Satan said to Jesus, "If you are God's Son, order these stones to turn to bread" (Matt. 4:3b, TEV). Jesus' hunger while fasting would naturally make the testing intense. "Deeper still was the tempting to be a bread messiah."[2] In

a country where not more than one-fifth of the land was arable under the best of conditions, and which was frequently plagued by extremes of drought and flood, bread was a precious commodity.[3] One sure way for Jesus to persuade people to follow him was to give them bread (John 6:5, 26).

To give men bread, though, would have meant bribing men to follow him. If Jesus were to be God's Messiah, he could not persuade men to follow him for what they could get out of him. Quoting the Scriptures, Jesus said to Satan, "Man shall not live by bread alone, but by every word that proceedeth out of the mouth of God" (Matt. 4:4).

2. Unsuccessful with the first approach, Satan tried again. This time he tried to get Jesus to be a "spectacular messiah."[4] Satan took Jesus to the pinnacle of the temple. At one corner of the temple "there was a sheer drop of four hundred and fifty feet into the valley . . . below. Why should Jesus not stand on that pinnacle, and leap down, and land unharmed in the valley beneath? That would startle men into following a man who could do a thing like that."[5]

If Jesus had adopted this course of action, the people would have never been satisfied. He would have had to produce greater and greater sensations to retain his power. Jesus would have no part of it. Again, quoting Scripture, Jesus said to Satan, "Thou shalt not tempt the Lord thy God" (Matt. 4:7).

3. Satan's third approach was to tempt Jesus by offering him the kingdoms of the world. Satan said: "All these things will I give thee, if thou wilt fall down and worship me" (Matt. 4:9). According to William Barclay, "What the tempter was saying was, 'Compromise! Come to terms with me! Don't pitch your demands quite so high! Wink just a little at evil and questionable things—and then people will follow

you in their hordes.' This was the temptation to come to terms with the world, instead of uncompromisingly presenting God's demands to the world."[6]

Jesus answered, "Get thee hence, Satan: for it is written, Thou shalt worship the Lord thy God, and him only shalt thou serve" (Matt. 4:10).

Jesus' duel with Satan was so spiritually taxing that God sent angels to minister to him (Mark 1:13; Matt. 4:11). By the time it was over, the principles for his ministry were established:

* He would not bribe people into following him.
* The way of sensationalism was not for him.
* He would not compromise his message.

THE CONTINUING STRUGGLE

I recently listened to a tape where two Christian leaders were discussing stress. They agreed that Jesus' life was one without stress. They said he had an unhurried, peaceful lifestyle. I couldn't help wondering if we had been reading the same Gospels, because Jesus' struggle wasn't over when the period of temptations ended (Luke 4:13; 22:28).

Although his ministry began in obscurity, within a year his popularity exploded. On various occasions he tried to withdraw from the crowds. Even when he attempted to go into Gentile territory where he thought he was not well known, people found him (Mark 7:24). The needy were always seeking him.

Jesus taught with authority and rebelled against the oral and scribal laws. The religious leaders constantly ridiculed him. They tried to discredit him or trap him in front of people. He was chased out of his own hometown. He lost his welcome in the synagogues. Even his family didn't understand him or his mission.

Jesus operated within a limited time frame, knowing his time was short and knowing he had much work to do. His close associates did not grasp the kind of kingdom he was trying to set up. When Peter tried to keep Jesus from taking the way of the cross, Jesus said to him words similar to what he said to Satan in the wilderness, "Satan be gone!" (see Matt. 16:23).

In his later ministry Jesus was hunted and watched. Toward the end of his life he was falsely accused and experienced unfair trials. He was betrayed by a coworker and deserted by his friends. And, of course, there was the fight of all fights with temptation that Jesus waged in Gethsemane when Satan sought to deflect him from the cross (Luke 22:42–44; Matt. 26:36–46; Mark 14:32–42).

Sounds stressful to me! Doing God's will was not a simple matter for Jesus.

THE "ALSO" FACTOR

In addition to *knowing* that Jesus struggled, we must *believe* that he did if we are to identify with him and learn how to pray about what we can't change. Giving mental assent to something is not the same as believing.

Jesus was human as well as divine. Many of us accept that statement on an intellectual level, but in our hearts we don't really believe it. We tend to believe that the divine, so evident in his life, kept Jesus free and lifted him above the circumstances of life.

To assume that his divinity kept him free of the struggles, the questionings, the fears, and the loneliness that are part of being human is to undermine the truth of the incarnation. He was human; the Word was made flesh (John 1:14). He was made like us.

If we don't believe Jesus struggled—if we don't acknowledge his humanity—then we will miss an important point of connection with him. We are more likely to imitate those with whom we feel a similarity or a kindred spirit. Identification leads to imitation.

We see this identification/imitation pattern in the apostle Peter's words to suffering believers, "For even hereunto were ye called: because Christ also suffered for us, leaving us an example, that ye should follow his steps" (1 Pet. 2:21).

Peter's use of the word *also* connects our suffering with Jesus'. It's a comfort to know that Jesus himself went through experiences like ours. It makes us feel like we are in the struggle together.

The word Peter used for *example* is very vivid. As Kenneth Wuest explains, "The word means literally 'writing under.' It was used of words given children to copy. . . . Sometimes it was used with reference to the act of tracing over written letters. . . . Just as a child slowly, with painstaking effort and close application, follows the shape of the letters of his teacher . . . "[7] so we should follow the example of Jesus.

Then Peter switched from the idea of a child tracing over the teacher's writing to following the footprints left by Jesus. Just as a child follows the footprints of a parent or older sibling in the sand, Peter encourages us to follow the footprints of Jesus. As we follow, we imitate him.

After her diving accident, it took Joni Eareckson Tada three years to connect with Jesus. Those years were filled with tears, bitterness, and violent questionings concerning her paralysis. In seconds, her life had changed from one of vigorous activity and independence to total helplessness and dependence. Philip Yancey, in his book *Where Is God When It Hurts,* describes the moment Joni identified with Jesus:

> Pain was streaking through her back in a way that is a unique torment to those paralyzed. Healthy persons can scratch an itch, squeeze an aching muscle, or flex a cramped foot. The paralyzed must lie still, defenseless, and feel the pain.
>
> Cindy, one of Joni's closest friends, was beside her bed, searching desperately for some way to encourage Joni. Finally, she clumsily blurted out, "Joni, Jesus knows how you feel—you aren't the only one—why, He was paralyzed too."
>
> Joni glared at her. "What? What are you talking about?"
>
> Cindy continued, "It's true. Remember He was nailed on a cross. His back was raw from beatings, and He must have yearned for a way to move to change positions, or redistribute His weight. But He couldn't. He was paralyzed by the nails."[8]

Joni found the connection "profoundly comforting."[9] Once she identified with Jesus, she could learn from him how to deal with what she could not change. They were "in it together." She said, "My focus changed from demanding an explanation from God to humbly depending on Him."[10]

MAKING THE CONNECTION

Many of us hold in our minds the picture of Jesus praying in the Garden of Gethsemane that is displayed in many churches and included in many Bibles. It is the picture where a halo encircles Jesus' head and light streams down from above. "He looks up serene and calm. The picture looks very holy, but it is not very real."[11]

"The halo makes Jesus different from us! So does the light. We have no halos. We are ordinary people. We have no light streaming at us from above, not in that way. . . . The moment Jesus receives a halo and light, He is no longer the human Jesus of the gospels. We destroy the whole gospel story. We deny that Jesus is man, actually man, so completely man that He *needs* to pray!"[12]

I believe Jesus wanted us to know he needed to pray. Otherwise he wouldn't have been so open about honestly praying in front of other people, something he did frequently.

I believe he also wanted us to know he experienced struggle, otherwise we wouldn't have known about his wilderness temptations. Jesus had been alone—no watchful observers were with him when this struggle occurred. No reporters or cameramen were recording the scene. The story could have come from nowhere else other than Jesus' own lips. Jesus himself must have told his disciples about this experience during some moment of intimate conversation. In telling it, he laid bare his heart and his soul so that those of us like Lois and Joni—who struggle with what we can't change—could connect with him. From there, we can learn from him, *if* we believe Jesus struggled and that he needed to pray.

MAKING YOUR WILL MINE

Have I come to realize I am struggling with something
I can't change?

In coping with what I can't change, who am I imitating?

What do Jesus and I have in common?

What is the difference between knowing Jesus struggled
and believing he did?

"Lord, I believe; help thou mine unbelief."[13]

PART II

THE SOLUTION

Walking with Jesus from His Baptism to the Cross

"Because the heart of our God is full of mercy
toward us,
the first light of Heaven shall come to visit us—
to shine on those who lie in darkness
and under the shadow of death,
and to guide our feet into the path of peace."

LUKE 1:78–79, PHILLIPS TRANSLATION

CHAPTER 4

GOING OR STAYING?

*The initial "Yes" to God in obedience, our "Thy
will be done" in a situation where what is asked of
us goes against the grain of all our natural
inclinations, does not mean the battle is over. We
have to go on saying the "Yes" at deeper and
deeper levels as we wrestle with the implications of
that obedience.*[1]

RONALD DUNN

"Do you remember the phone call we've been waiting for, the one that would tell us the cross for the top of our church had arrived?" asked the pastor. "Well, the call came Friday night."

Murmurs and chuckles rippled through the congregation. On Friday night, it had snowed.

"It had been snowing a couple of hours and darkness was settling in when I received the call. The truck driver said, 'I have your cross. I must quickly unload it and be on my way. Where is the church?'

"I told him our church was located north of town right

off the main highway. I said, 'You'll easily spot it because it sits on top of a high hill. I'll meet you at the bottom of the hill.'

"When I arrived, I got into the cab with the driver. He tried to drive the truck up the hill, but the steep hill was too slick from the fresh snow. We talked about what to do and decided to carry the cross.

"I carried the small box of attachments and the truck driver carried the cross. It was as tall as he was, and he hoisted it over his shoulder. It was snowing too hard to make conversation, so we walked in silence. In the fading daylight, I watched the driver ahead of me slip and stumble with the bulky cross. Immediately, my thoughts turned to Jesus and his walk to Calvary. I'll admit I had never really thought about what that walk must have been like for him."

As the pastor went on sharing the insight he gained, I thought, *I wish I could have an experience like that.* I had a hunch that something dramatic, something where I could actually put myself in Jesus' place for awhile, would draw me closer to him. Like the apostle Paul, I wanted "to *know* Christ and the power of his resurrection and the fellowship of sharing in his sufferings" (Phil. 3:10, NIV, emphasis added).

It was not Paul's aim to know *about* Christ;[2] Paul had been a believer for many years when he expressed this desire. Paul's aim was to progressively become more deeply and intimately acquainted with Jesus. The pastor's story helped me to realize that I wanted the same thing.

Once I recognized this, I should have immediately pursued ways to know Jesus better, but I didn't. Like many good sermon listeners, my motivation disappeared once I left the church.

Maybe it was because at the time I was still living in the anything-can-be-changed stage of life. Later, when I discovered that everything in life can't be changed, I took hold of Jesus' hand and began walking with him.

Being a "pray-er" by nature and by choice, my walk naturally focused on Jesus' prayer life. Where did he pray? When did he pray? What led him to pray? What were his requests? How did he phrase them? Finding the answers to these questions would help me know Jesus more intimately.

JESUS' PRAYER LIFE

Examining anyone's prayer life is hard. How can we really be certain about the thought processes of another individual, even a contemporary, even a loved one? Entering the mind of someone who lived two thousand years ago and who was both God and man is even more difficult. Walking with Jesus takes effort.

SOME ANALYSIS REQUIRED

Where Jesus' actual prayers are recorded in the Bible, we know exactly what he prayed for. At other times, though, the object of his prayer is not stated; it is inferred by the circumstances. Here our judgment must enter in. That is, we must determine the object of prayer by analyzing the incident, what happened before Jesus prayed and what happened afterwards.

Let's see how this process of inference works in Mark 1:35, the first recorded incident of Jesus' praying after his baptism and his temptations in the wilderness.[3]

WHAT HAPPENED BEFORE JESUS PRAYED

The first year of Jesus' ministry was mostly spent in Judea where John the Baptist preached and baptized. "After John had been put in prison, Jesus went to Galilee and

preached the Good News from God" (Mark 1:14, TEV).
While there, his popularity exploded.

In the synagogue in Capernaum, Jesus amazed the people by the way he taught (Mark 1:22). He wasn't like the scribes; Jesus taught with authority.

The people were dumbfounded when he cast out an unclean spirit (Mark 1:25–26). "This man has authority to give orders to the evil spirits, and they obey him!" (Mark 1:27b, TEV).

News about Jesus and his ability spread quickly (Mark 1:28). Then Jesus healed Simon Peter's mother-in-law (Mark 1:31), and that was the match that ignited the explosion. By sundown, "people brought to Jesus all the sick and those who had demons. All the people of the town gathered in front of the house" (Mark 1:32b–33, TEV) of Simon Peter and Andrew.

THE INCIDENT OF PRAYER

The next morning "rising up a great while before day, he went out, and departed into a solitary place, and there prayed" (Mark 1:35).

According to Curtis C. Mitchell, who did a careful word study of Jesus' prayer life, "The expressions 'rising up' and 'went out' grammatically indicate a decisive action, not simply an attitude."[4] The specific description of the place as "solitary" indicates he wanted to avoid people and other distractions. "Thus both the *time* and the *place* seem to indicate a deliberate attempt on the part of Christ to get alone and pray. . . . In all probability it was a prayer session of some length, because a man would hardly arise at such an inconvenient hour to trudge out into the desert for a few moments of prayer."[5]

When Simon Peter and those with him awoke, they discovered that Jesus had disappeared. They went searching for him (Mark 1:36). When they spotted Jesus, they said, "Everyone is looking for you" (Mark 1:37c, TEV). When they found Jesus, they tried to keep him from leaving their area (Luke 4:42).

WHAT HAPPENED AFTERWARDS

Jesus "read their hearts."[6] He knew the people were going to try to keep him from leaving. The multitude wanted to keep him in their place, concerned about their locality only.

Jesus said that he must go on to the other villages. "I have to preach in them also, because that is why I came" (Mark 1:38b, TEV).

"So he traveled all over Galilee, preaching in the synagogues and driving out demons" (Mark 1:39, TEV).

THE INFERENCE

When we pull together the press of the crowd, the escape to a solitary place, and Jesus' decision to leave, the inference is that Jesus prayed because he needed God's guidance.

Should he go or should he stay? The people of Capernaum were needy people; should he localize his ministry and stay there? It was a bustling city of many people. Wouldn't that be a large enough ministry area? Or, should he go to other areas? What did God want him to do?

Were numerous healings consistent with his mission? Jesus' popularity in Capernaum was due largely to the miracles he produced. As Curtis Mitchell states, "To be sure, healing had its place as a means of authenticating His

Person and message. However, it was not intended to become an end in itself, which was exactly what the people apparently desired."[7] Were the people interested only in his miracles? If he stayed, would he be able to lead them on to deeper spiritual truths? What did God want him to do?

While Jesus knew his broad purpose and principles through his baptism and his temptations, he continued to need God's guidance about the specifics. If that were not the case, Jesus would have been a mere robot or a puppet. He was a thinking person, a person who could be tempted, a person who interacted with people and responded to their needs, therefore he needed to continually consult God.

Through prayer, Jesus came to understand clearly what the specifics were at this time. He understood that he must leave the miracle-seeking multitude and go to other places. By the time Simon Peter and the others arrived, Jesus had his answer. He said, "I must preach the Good News of the Kingdom of God in other towns also, because that is what God sent me to do' " (Luke 4:43, TEV). He could say decisively and firmly what he was going to do because he had prayed.

MAKING THE CONNECTION

Barbara (from chap. 1) knew just enough about holiness to resist it. When God spoke to her at the student retreat, her initial response was, "Oh, God, please don't ask me to change." Resigning herself to what she figured was inevitable (*God always wins, doesn't he?*), Barbara verbally committed herself to changing her lifestyle in the retreat's closing commitment service.

On the ride back to campus, Barbara realized she didn't

know much about holiness. She knew the basic concept was one of separateness. Did that mean she would have to separate herself from all her non-Christian friends? Would she have to dress differently? Change her vocabulary? Change her habits? Would she be lonely? Would she be peculiar? Overwhelmed by the possibilities, Barbara buried her face in her hands. She thought, *What have I gotten myself into! I'll never be able to live a holy life.*

Barbara needed specifics about doing God's will just as Jesus did. To receive guidance, she had to be just as deliberate as he was.

Back at the dormitory, Barbara set her alarm for 5:00 A.M. When the alarm went off the next morning, she reluctantly crawled out of her warm bed. Careful not to disturb her roommate, she grabbed her Bible and blanket and slipped out of her room. In the lounge, while other students were sleeping, Barbara opened God's Word and opened her heart to discovering how he wanted her to live.

Morning after morning she continued this pattern. Many a morning Barbara wanted to pull the covers close and avoid the loneliness of the lounge at 5 A.M. Yet on those mornings she thought of Jesus. She wondered if it had been hard for him to leave Capernaum while everyone else was asleep. When she had been up late studying for a test the night before, she wondered about Jesus' exhaustion from his busy day. Had it been hard for him to get up long before daylight when his body was tired from the previous day's activities?

Thinking of Jesus gave Barbara the determination and inspiration she needed to meet God for guidance in that lounge at the end of the hall. And in those moments, God spoke to her and showed her what he wanted. She received the guidance she needed—and more:

* God strengthened Barbara's resolve to be different; he gave her the courage to be his person.
* At first she looked upon God's call to holiness as a bondage, but as she disciplined herself to be like Jesus, she experienced freedom. Now, she could be her authentic self instead of being a chameleon trying to please everyone.
* She grew closer to Jesus. He had been her Savior ever since she became a Christian as a child, but now he was also her friend.
* She experienced spiritual power. As she took on the nature of Jesus, she began to see others through his eyes. She now saw her sophisticated friends as spiritually needy, and she reached out to help them instead of trying to impress them.

When Barbara looks back on the guidance, freedom, intimacy, and power she discovered from identifying with and imitating Jesus, she wonders why she ever bristled at living by God's unchangeable standards.

Maybe the work involved had something to do with it. To walk with Jesus, to identify with him and to imitate him, requires effort. Examining his prayer life even requires effort because we must pull together and analyze information.

Motivation may also have something to do with it. Some of us aren't motivated to walk with Jesus until we come up against something we can't change. I wasn't. You may not be at that place; your options are still wide open. No matter where we find ourselves, Jesus extends the invitation to us, "Follow me." The question before us is, will we go or will we stay? Will we go forward to seek to know him more fully or will we stay where we are?

MAKING YOUR WILL MINE

What kind of mental work is necessary to understanding Jesus' prayers?

How can I become more deeply and intimately acquainted with Jesus?

How can I discover the specifics of doing God's will?

*"In the morning, O Lord, you hear my voice;
in the morning I lay my requests before you
and wait in expectation."*[8]

CHAPTER 5

SEEKING HELP IN LONELY PLACES

We who live in the quiet places have the
opportunity to become acquainted with ourselves,
to think our own thoughts and live our own lives
in a way that is not possible for those who are
keeping up with the crowd.[1]

LAURA INGALLS WILDER

After Jesus left Capernaum, he preached and healed in other Galilean cities. Excitement surrounded him again when he healed a man with a very serious case of leprosy (Luke 5:12–13).

When the leper saw Jesus, "he threw himself down and begged him, 'Sir, if you want to, you can make me clean!' " (Luke 5:12b, TEV).

"Jesus reached out and touched him. 'I do want to,' he answered. 'Be clean!' At once the disease left the man" (Luke 5:13, TEV).

Jesus sternly said to him, "Don't tell this to anyone"

(Mark 1:44a, TEV). Jesus may have done this to minimize rumors spreading about him. "Galilee was a hotbed of messianic hope;"[2] the people wanted a revolutionary deliverer. Jesus did not want to link himself with that kind of expectation.

The cured leper ignored Jesus' instructions. He spread the news of his healing everywhere (Mark 1:45). Leprosy was a dreaded and loathsome disease, so the news that a serious case was healed spread quickly. Consequently, "great multitudes came together to hear, and to be healed by him of their infirmities" (Luke 5:15).

We would expect Jesus to rejoice at the sight of the gathering crowd. What an opportunity to heal and to help many people! Instead, "he withdrew himself into the wilderness, and prayed" (Luke 5:16).

According to Curtis C. Mitchell, "The word *withdrew* grammatically describes a *habitual action* rather than a *single act*."[3] The verse is translated this way in some versions of the Bible (TEV and NIV). A pattern of withdrawal is implied, and a broad look at his prayer life verifies it:

* He withdrew to the wilderness to seek guidance about localizing his ministry (described in chap. 4).
* He withdrew after people gathered following the healing of the leper (this chapter).
* He withdrew before he chose his apostles (next chapter).
* He withdrew when the crowd wanted to make him king (chap. 7).
* With three companions, he sought the silence of a lonely mountain as the stage for his transfiguration (chap. 9).

* As he prepared for his death, he sought the solitude of the Garden of Gethsemane (chap. 12).

The crowds, wild with enthusiasm over Christ's miraculous powers, continually gathered around him day after day, while Jesus slipped away from them to pray.

WHERE DID JESUS GO?

The places to which Jesus went indicate that he needed to be alone:

* "Into the desert" (Matt. 4:1; Mark 1:12; Luke 4:1, TEV) or "the wilderness" (KJV). These were uninhabited regions.
* "Out of town to a lonely place" (Mark 1:35, TEV) or "a solitary place" (KJV).
* "The wilderness" (Luke 5:16, KJV) or "to lonely places" (TEV).
* "Up a hill" (Luke 6:12, TEV) or "out into a mountain" (KJV).
* "Departed into a mountain to pray" (Mark 6:46, KJV), "to a hill to pray" (TEV), or "up on a mountainside" (NIV).
* "Into a deserted place by ship privately" (Mark 6:32, KJV) or "by themselves to a lonely place" (TEV).
* "Left there in a boat and went to a lonely place" (Matt. 14:13, TEV) or "into a deserted place" (KJV).

THE BENEFITS OF LONELY PLACES

What did solitude do for Jesus and what can it do for us?
1. *Solitude offers privacy for dealing with emotions.*

When Jesus heard the news about the martyrdom of John the Baptist, he left the crowd and went by boat to a lonely place (Matt. 14:13). Through John's ministry Jesus had been baptized and had received direction for his own work in the world. John's death was a sobering reminder to Jesus that he, too, would suffer a similar fate. Facing his grief over the loss of a ministry colleague and the realization of the danger he was facing called for solitude.

Emotions accompany things we can't change. Some of those emotions can be very strong—too strong to share even with friends. Or, we may be conscious that others are watching us, waiting to see how we are going to respond. We don't need this kind of scrutinizing when we are struggling to make adjustments. Solitude gives us a place to deal with our emotions apart from watchful eyes and where we can be free to express them.

In his book *A Grace Disguised,* Gerald L. Sittser, a college teacher who lost his mother, his wife, and a daughter in an automobile accident, described how solitude helped him to handle his loss. His moments of solitude were late in the evening, after his remaining children were in bed. He writes, "Sometimes I listened to music—mostly requiems, Gregorian chants, and other choral works; and sometimes I wrote in my journal or read good books. But mostly I sat in my rocking chair and stared into space, reliving the accident and remembering the people I lost. I felt anguish in my soul and cried bitter tears."[4]

Sittser said, "This nightly solitude, as painful and demanding as it was, became sacred to me because it allowed time for genuine mourning and intense reflection."[5]

2. *Solitude facilitates thinking.* Jesus needed a lonely place, without the presence of people and their continual interruptions, to sort out his thoughts and to seek God's guidance.

When we struggle with something we can't change, we may be bombarded by swirling thoughts. The thoughts and their intensity will vary depending on the individual and what can't be changed. Solitude provides a climate for sorting out those thoughts.

When Peggy (from chap. 1) was diagnosed with scleroderma, she was so dismayed by the diagnosis that she thought about taking her life. She wondered what effects the illness would have on her children and her husband, and she wondered what God's will for her was.

Even though Peggy had a regular quiet time of prayer and Bible study, those moments weren't long enough to sort out her questions. She worked full-time and was concerned about being late for work. She needed unhurried time but couldn't find that because her family was planning a major long-distance move.

Peggy said, "When we moved, I knew I wouldn't have to work outside the home for a while. I promised myself . . . I'd take the time to really work through this disease thing with God."[6]

Peggy used the lonely days following their move—when she wasn't interrupted by phone calls or activities and when her life was not highly scheduled—to sort out her thoughts and to seek God's guidance.

When we leave the crowded city and head for a nature preserve, when we climb a mountain and change our view, when we escape the noises of radios and televisions, our breathing slows, our heart stops beating so rapidly, and our thinking improves. Apart from distractions, we have a keener quality of attention that helps us examine alternatives and find solutions.

3. *Solitude improves listening.* Once we sort out our thoughts, we need God's guidance on how to proceed. That requires communication.

While God spoke audibly to Jesus on three occasions, Jesus' rising before dawn to pray and his spending nights in prayer implies that communion with God frequently requires unhurried quiet. Communion with God requires dialogue—speaking, listening, waiting, and receiving. While this can be done in the presence of distractions, it is easier to listen and to receive when we are not distracted and when we are not in a hurry.

David Hazard, the editor of a devotional series drawn from classic Christian writings, writes, "Throughout Scripture and church history, God has always shown up and spoken His mind whenever humans have taken seriously His call to quiet."[7] In a lonely place, unhurried by the demands of people or by our schedules, our receptivity for hearing God's voice is heightened.

4. *Solitude refreshes.* Once Jesus became popular in Galilee, he was rarely without a crowd around him.

* When he was on his way to Jairus's house, so many people were going along with Jesus that they crowded him from every side (Mark 5:24).
* He was forced to preach from a borrowed boat in order to distance himself from the growing crowd on the shore (Matt. 13:2).
* The paralytic's friends lowered him through a hole in the roof because of the crowd surrounding Jesus (Mark 2:4).
* When the apostles returned from their mission assignment, they tried to tell Jesus about it, but so many people were coming and going that they didn't even have time to eat (Mark 6:31).
* When Jesus tried to retreat with the apostles for training and rest, he didn't want anyone to know

where they were, but Jesus could not be hidden (Mark 7:24).

The demands upon Jesus' sympathy and compassion were unrelenting. To continue to respond to the many pressing needs around him was emotionally and spiritually draining. "Every time Jesus healed anyone it took something out of Him."[8] *The Interpreter's Bible* states, "In order that he might respond to the pitiful thirst for help of those who flocked to him, he had to separate himself from time to time that through communion with his Father the reservoirs of his own soul might be filled again from the fountains that were on high."[9]

When we seek out the lonely places, when we commune with God there, we give him the opportunity to renew our resources. Sittser said his own nighttime solitude ". . . gave me freedom during the day to invest my energy into teaching and caring for my children. I struggled with exhaustion. . . . But somehow I found the strength—God's gift to me . . . to carry on."[10]

When we seek the lonely places, we have an opportune place and time to deal with our thoughts and emotions, to gain refreshment and strength, and to hear God's voice.

WHY ARE WE HESITANT?

Despite the benefits of solitary time with God, some of us may be reluctant to visit lonely places. We hesitate for a variety of reasons.

* We may be so hurt over what has happened to us—what it is that we can't change—that we want to avoid God. We don't want to hear his voice. We may not say so out loud, but we find him at fault for what happened.

* We may not want to express or acknowledge our emotions. We may pride ourselves on being unemotional, or we may be afraid of expressing emotions. Releasing grief and anger can be unpleasant and even agonizing.

* We may be afraid the solitude will be painful, and it may be, particularly at first. Sittser described it as descending "into the darkness alone."[11]

* We may be on a treadmill of nonstop activity, and we cannot see how we can get off, even if it is for just a day, or two, or a few hours. Faxes are coming in, mail is arriving, the phone is ringing, E-mail messages are piling up. If we take time out, we will get behind.

* Perhaps we feel that to seek solitude is to face being alone, something that petrifies many people, so we surround ourselves with noise and people.

* We may insist we have no place to be alone. Our space is crowded. Someone is always around.

* While we acknowledge that solitude helped Jesus, we may think, "It really wouldn't help me." Yet that's exactly what Satan would have us think. He would like for us to miss out on the benefits of solitude.

To reap the benefits, we may have to be just as deliberate and persevering as Jesus was. The people who pursued him were very aggressive. They seemed to have an uncanny sense for knowing where he was and how to find him. They were ever present with their many needs—needs I'm sure Jesus didn't want to ignore; although at times, he did. We may have to be just as deliberate to sort out our thoughts and feelings, to commune with God and to give him a channel to guide us and refresh us. The results will be worth it, and you will be glad you visited the lonely places.

MAKING YOUR WILL MINE

As I deal with what I can't change, my thoughts are:

My feelings are:

Where are some lonely places I can use to commune with God?

What is preventing me from visiting those places?

I will set an appointment for time alone with God at _____ .

"Silently now I wait for Thee,
Ready, my God, Thy will to see."[12]

CHAPTER 6

WHAT DO I DO?

We do not always have the freedom to choose the
roles we must play in life, but we can choose how
we are going to play the roles we have been given.[1]

GERALD L. SITTSER

Choices accompany things we can't change. That combination sounds incongruous, doesn't it? Choices and "can't" don't seem to go together—but they do. When we come up against something unchangeable, we will have decisions to make.

JESUS FACED CHOICES

When Jesus heard God's voice at his baptism, he knew he was God's chosen Messiah. He knew the way for him was the way of the cross. While he could not change that destiny, he did have many decisions to make as he interpreted what it meant to be the Messiah.

A DEVELOPING CRISIS

The task of being the Messiah included showing what God really wanted in the way of worship and obedience. Religion for many Jews had become a matter of rules and regulations. Nowhere was this more true than in the observance of the Sabbath.

Honoring the seventh day of the week by not working "had developed into a very complicated and burdensome chore. The Mosaic restrictions had been elaborated and multiplied until they numbered into the hundreds."[2] These oral restrictions made the keeping of the Sabbath practically impossible. What's more, they destroyed the spirit of the Sabbath.[3]

Jesus could not tolerate the unnumbered and ridiculous regulations. "Real religion meant more than the observance of these regulations."[4] Jesus openly challenged the system, even healing a man whose condition could have waited until another day. Opposition to Jesus naturally followed.

Filled with rage at Jesus' perceived abuse of the Sabbath, the Pharisees began to discuss among themselves what they would do to Jesus (Luke 6:11). They entered into what was for them an "unholy alliance" with a secular group called Herodians. Together they made plans to kill Jesus (Mark 3:6). The intensity of the opposition reminded Jesus that time was running out.

THE CRUCIAL CHOICE

There was so much Jesus wanted to say, to teach, and to do. He wanted the people to know what God really wanted and what he was like. Jesus wanted to make sure his message continued after his death.

If only he could reach people in more places, but he could only be in one place at a time. His voice could reach only a limited number of people. In that day there were no means of mass communication. If any message was presented to people, it was presented personally.

If Jesus' work was to branch out—and go on—Jesus needed helpers to accompany him, to strengthen his ministry (Mark 3:14b). He needed preachers (Mark 3:14c) to spread his message and to guarantee its existence after he was gone. The Gospel of Luke describes how Jesus responded to this need: "In these days he went out into the hills to pray; and all night he continued in prayer to God. And when it was day, he called his disciples, and chose from them twelve, whom he named apostles" (Luke 6:12–13, RSV).

"Though the passage does not state in so many words the purpose for this deliberate, all-night prayer vigil, all commentators unite in recognizing that it was in some manner associated with the decision . . ."[5] to choose the twelve apostles. The choice was so crucial that it had to be faced in long hours of effort in order to know whom to select.

THE TIME INVOLVED

The word translated "all night" is a medical term. It was used in the Greek to describe the all-night vigil of a doctor as he waited at the bedside of a patient. The original word gives a "picture of urgency, earnestness, and intensity."[6] Jesus did not go out for a hike up the mountain and then decide it would be nice to pray. "His withdrawal into the hills to pray all night reflected the burden which he carried."[7]

"Alone and apart from all the distractions of the world below, Jesus let his mind and soul commune with God."[8] He sought illumination and guidance. By morning he had his answer. He called his disciples to him and chose twelve men from among them to be apostles. He chose them to strengthen his ministry and to see that it continued after his death. Through prayer Jesus made a choice that enabled his ministry to expand beyond the limitations of space and time.

With some choices that accompany what we can't change, we will need to maintain a vigil of prayer just as Jesus did. Decisions that are crucial, involving far-reaching consequences, may need hours of prayer to discover God's will. Maintaining a vigil doesn't necessarily mean spending one night in prayer, but it does mean spending *time* in prayer. We will need time to identify our choices, look at the alternatives, consider their consequences and listen for God's answer.

IDENTIFYING OUR CHOICES

Leah had urgent choices to make when her husband was killed in a freak hunting accident. At the time, Leah was a stay-at-home pastor's wife with two small children. Her husband's death meant the loss of their income and the parsonage they had lived in for four years. In one blow she lost her husband, her home, and her income. While trying to come to grips with her husband's death, Leah had to figure out where she and the children were going to live and how they were going to pay for it. She had to make choices about a job, about childcare, and about housing.

Sometimes the choices that accompany what we can't change will not be as obvious as Leah's. They won't have

WHAT DO I DO?

an urgency to them like the need for money, shelter, child-care, etc. They may be more nebulous choices, such as:

* Will I accept or reject what I cannot change?
* Will I define what happened as the end or a new beginning?
* Will I hold on to the person I was or will I grow with the experience?

The impact of what we can't change may leave us feeling like we have no choices. Or, we may get bogged down emotionally. Our grief, resentment, anger, or despair may blind us to our choices. We may need to pray, "Father, I feel trapped and I feel cheated. Open my eyes to possibilities. Help me to see the choices I have."

Identifying our choices is important. The power to choose gives us the ability to transcend our circumstances and to grow and to gain from them. Otherwise we may begin to see ourselves as victims and remain stuck in the mire of what we cannot change.

LOOKING AT THE ALTERNATIVES

What Leah really wanted was to go back to the way life was when her husband was alive. But people kept asking her, "What are you going to do? Where are you going to go?" Then the church trustees told her she needed to be out of the parsonage in six months. While they were kind in how they said it, and Leah understood their need for a time limit, she felt an increasing sense of doom. She had to make choices whether she wanted to or not.

Because of her small children, Leah couldn't withdraw to the hills for an overnight prayer vigil, but she could get up early before her children were awake. In the early morning quiet, she verbalized her needs for housing, for a job, and for childcare. Taking a pencil and paper, she listed various alternatives as they came to her. Seeing the alternatives lifted her spirits.

The next morning she gathered more strength as she prayed over each alternative. She eliminated some and added others. Morning by morning she prayerfully pared the list down to those that seemed reasonable and appropriate.

Jesus, too, had alternatives to consider. We don't usually think about them because the concept of the twelve apostles is so set in our minds and because the number is symbolically linked to the twelve tribes of Israel. Some possibilities include:

* He could have written a book to enlarge and preserve his ministry.
* He could have chosen other men than those he chose.
* He could have chosen more or fewer men.
* He could have chosen women.

CONSIDERING THE CONSEQUENCES

Each alternative and its consequences need to be carefully considered before a choice is made. Jesus must have asked many questions as he considered his choices. Who would he choose as disciples? Out of all his disciples, who would be willing to identify their life with his? The crowds might be there one day and gone the next. Followers might fluctuate and be spasmodic in their attachment to Jesus, but he needed helpers who were dependable. Which ones would be faithful over the long haul? Who would be will-

ing to travel and to be homeless? Which ones were courageous enough to identify with a rebel?

We too must think about possible consequences, or we
might end up surprised at God's answer. We might even be
tempted to be angry with him.

Sometimes in the emotional turmoil of struggling with
something we can't change, we long for a perfect answer to
prayer—an answer that spells *end of struggle*. If the answer
we receive involves more struggle, we may become angry
with God. More growth was the last thing we wanted. Comfort is what we had in mind when we prayed.

God is trustworthy, so we don't have to be afraid of his
answers, but we may be surprised by them. The men God
led Jesus to choose had all kinds of faults. Some of them
were given to emotional outbursts. Some argued about positions of honor. One denied knowing Jesus, and another
betrayed him. God's answer did not spell *end of struggle*
for Jesus, but God's answer was sufficient. These ordinary
men, with their faults, strengthened Jesus' ministry. Through
them, Jesus' message survived, as the Book of Acts reveals.

LISTENING TO GOD

I can't imagine Jesus petitioning God with words all
night long. As he considered the urgency of his need, as he
looked at the alternatives before him, as he considered their
consequences, he listened. Listening is the most important
element in the choice-making prayer vigil. It is in listening
that we receive God's answer. It's a moment worth waiting
for, because then we can proceed with confidence.

Some of Leah's friends grew impatient with her when
she didn't take the jobs that became available in their community. But Leah knew they weren't the jobs God had for

her. In her early morning prayer vigil, God showed her the kind of job she needed, so she held out for that kind of job. She found it two weeks before she was to be out of the parsonage.

I don't understood why a vigil is sometimes required to receive God's answer. It looks like, if our hearts are sincere, we could just ask God what to do, and he would tell us. On occasion we may actually receive his instructions that easily, but more often the process takes time. It's almost as if the process itself is important. Maybe it is. As we pray, we unfold ourselves, opening our will to his leadership. We sift and weigh, changing our perspective to match God's perspective. Our vision widens; our hope rises. We pray on, listening until the moment comes when we know we have God's answer.

MAKING YOUR WILL MINE

What choice or choices do I have regarding
what I can't change?

What are the alternatives that comprise each choice?

What are the consequences of each alternative?

"Lord, what wilt thou have me to do?"[9]

CHAPTER 7

BEING FAITHFUL REGARDLESS

Weapons which the Christian can use . . . are steadfastness and loyalty. The word for steadfastness is that great word hupomone, *which does not simply mean passively bearing things; it means courageously accepting the worst that life can do, and turning it into glory. The word for loyalty is* pistis, *and it means that fidelity which will never waver in its utter devotion to its Master and its Lord.*[1]

WILLIAM BARCLAY

When my children were small, I often read to them a story about Tootle, a small locomotive.[2] Tootle attended a school for locomotives so he could became the Flyer train between New York and Chicago. He could never be a good train, let alone the Flyer, unless he made an A+ in the course called, "Staying on the Rails No Matter What."

One day while Tootle was practicing staying on the rails, a strong black horse came running across the meadow. "Race you to the river," he shouted. Tootle accepted the challenge, left the track, and raced the horse through the meadow. Once Tootle discovered how nice it was in the meadow, he was easily distracted by buttercups, a frog, and daisies.

As my children wondered how Tootle was ever going to learn to stay on the rails, I thought of how Christians have to learn the same lesson. We are often tempted to get off the narrow "way, which leadeth unto life" (Matt. 7:14). This occurs for various reasons:

* Sometimes God's call is clear and precise initially, and we know exactly what to do. But after we have been doing it for awhile, the call may lose some of its clarity as we deal with its day-by-day challenges. At that point we may look around, see what others are doing, and wonder if we are on the right track.

* The Christian life involves friction. To be righteous in an unrighteous world is to encounter resistance. We may get weary of the continual resistance and want to bail out.

* God may not act in accordance with what we believe about him. As we study the Bible, as we read what others write, and as we listen to what others say, we develop assumptions about God. When God does something not in accordance with our assumptions, we are thrown for a loop. The disappointment may be so keen that we want to give up.

* Satan and his forces are constantly at work to detract us from doing what is right. Sometimes his efforts are as obvious as the strong black horse challenging Tootle to a race—what we would label as out-and-out evil. But other times Satan's efforts aren't as discernible. Our "good" activities (the buttercups and daisies of our lives) can have distractions lurking in them. Although Satan's work is

more subtle and deceptive here, it can distract us just the same.

THE CONTINUED TEMPTING OF JESUS

We can easily recognize Satan's work when we read about how he confronted Jesus in the wilderness (chap. 3). His efforts were obvious as he tempted Jesus to give people bread to get them to follow him. At the time, Jesus rejected that way of power. Later, however, the temptation came back, and this time Satan's efforts weren't as obvious. Jesus wasn't alone in the wilderness. He was busy doing good and having a successful ministry of teaching and healing.

THE RELENTLESS CROWD

After Jesus chose the twelve apostles, he began training them. He sent them out two by two to minister on their own. When they returned, they were ready to talk. They wanted to share their experiences with Jesus. People, though, clamored around them. "There were so many people coming and going that Jesus and his disciples didn't even have time to eat" (Mark 6:31, TEV).

Jesus said, "Let us go off by ourselves to some place where we will be alone and you can rest a while" (Mark 6:31b, TEV). They got into a boat and headed "to a lonely place" (Mark 6:32b, TEV).

Seeing the boat set sail, the people easily deduced where it was going. "At this particular place it was four miles across the lake by boat and ten miles round the top of the lake on foot. On a windless day, or with a contrary wind, a boat might take some time to make the passage, and an energetic person could walk round the top of the lake and be there before the boat arrived."[3] In this case, it was not an energetic person, but an energetic crowd! When Jesus and his men stepped out of the boat, the very crowd from which they had sought relief was waiting for them.

The crowd pursued Jesus "because they saw his miracles which he did on them that were diseased" (John 6:2). Their intent was to get something from him. They wanted him to heal their sick; they wanted to see his dazzling miracles.

Instead of being annoyed, Jesus' heart was filled with compassion for them (Matt. 14:14). He saw them as "sheep not having a shepherd" (Mark 6:34), and he began to teach them (Mark 6:34) and to heal their sick (Matt. 14:14c).

"The day began to wear away" (Luke 9:12a). The crowd of more than five thousand people became hungry, and Jesus miraculously provided food for them with five loaves and two fish. This miracle triggered tremendous excitement. So far, they hadn't seen anything like this! The people concluded, "Surely this is the Prophet who was to come to the world! (John 6:14b, TEV)."

The Jews were waiting for the prophet who would be like Moses. Moses had said, "The Lord thy God will raise up unto thee a Prophet from the midst of thee, of thy brethren, like unto me; unto him ye shall hearken" (Deut. 18:15). Through Moses, God had miraculously provided bread from heaven (manna). Now, here was Jesus miraculously providing bread.

The people wanted a leader like Moses—someone to give them free food and political deliverance.[4] Jesus was just the person; he would make a terrific king. They were so certain of this, they were ready to make him king by force (John 6:15).

THE KINGDOM WITHOUT THE CROSS

Jesus could have made a convincing argument for giving in to the crowd. For example:

* Couldn't he do a lot of good for the people, even for God, by becoming a political Messiah?
* What's wrong with using miraculous power to deliver people from the dominion of the Romans? They are God's people; they deserve to be free.
* What's wrong with reducing hunger and curing ills? God does not want people to be hungry or to suffer unnecessarily.

What a temptation this must have been for Jesus! "Here was an opportunity to be king apart from suffering, apart from the cross."[5]

Subtly and deceptively through needy people, Satan was trying to detract Jesus from the path of suffering and the cross. How did Jesus keep from getting off course?

DELIBERATE, PRAYERFUL ACTION

First, Jesus made the disciples get into a boat and go on ahead to the other side of the lake (Matt. 14:22). The fever of a crowd is contagious. Jesus did not want the disciples infected with the "Make Jesus King" campaign. That would have added to the group's momentum and to the pressure on him.

Next, he calmed the crowd, told them good-bye, and sent them away. Then he went up into the mountain to pray (Matt. 14:23). Away from the clamor, the constant movement, the chatter, and the needs of the crowd, Jesus communed with God.

How do we know Jesus was helped by this? He returned to the crowd the next day with a "singleness of a heart intent only on God's will and made new in God's power."[6] This is obvious in the courageous and direct way Jesus related to the crowd after his time of prayer.

When they caught up with Jesus in Capernaum (John 6:24), he said, "I tell you the truth: you are looking for me because you ate the bread and had all you wanted, not because you understood my works of power. Do not work for food that spoils; instead, work for the food that lasts for eternal life. This food the Son of Man will give you, because God, the Father, has put his mark of approval on him" (John 6:26–27, TEV).

Revealing himself as the "bread of life" was a real crowd separator. The people didn't like the idea of spiritual bread. Many decided Jesus' teaching was just too hard (John 6:60a), and others refused to follow him any longer (John 6:66). Nevertheless, Jesus stayed on track. Praying enabled him to resist Satan's temptation.

The way Jesus responded to the crowd's wanting to make him king shouldn't surprise us. He frequently withdrew for prayer. It is the most obvious pattern in his prayer life.

The pattern itself has power. When this temptation came to Jesus, he did not have to stop and ask, "How should I handle this?" Joachim Jeremias says that the phrase "as his custom was" in Luke 4:16 may mean not only that Jesus regularly attended Sabbath worship but also that he prayed regularly.[7] As a devout member of the Jewish community, it is likely that Jesus faithfully observed their custom of praying three times a day. These established times of prayer "provided a fabric of discipline" to his prayer life.[8] The pattern of prayer was so ingrained in Jesus that his natural response to distractions was to withdraw for prayer.

Without a pattern of withdrawals in our life, we might be tempted to yield to distractions when they occur. The nature of distractions are such that they discourage us from praying. But if we are in the habit of praying, we will pray even when we don't feel like it. We will communicate with God even when we are disappointed and confused about his actions. We will stay faithful regardless of the circumstances.

THE POWER OF HABIT

My husband was unhappy in his job at a community college in a large city. Bob wanted to look for another job, but I didn't want to move. We lived near a large theological library where I had access to thousands of books. The view from my desk was a tree-filled ravine with all its natural beauties. I drew inspiration from the trees and wildlife. I thought I had a perfect situation as a writer.

Bob persisted. After much discussion, we agreed to pray, "Father, if it is your will for Bob to get another job, we pray that you will open the door. We'll not contact any employment agencies. If a new job comes along, it will be totally your doing."

After several months of praying this way, Bob received a phone call from a major Christian university in another state. They had an administrative opening. To Bob and me that call might as well have been from God himself! After several interviews Bob was offered the job, and we moved.

The move was difficult for me, and so was the subsequent adjustment. Through it all, I at least had the comfort of believing that we were doing God's will. We had prayed, and God had opened the door. We trusted him. In time, I would adjust.

Bob had been on his new job about six months when he said to me, "I made a mistake in taking this job."

I wanted to say, "You what? How could you have made a mistake when we prayed about this? How could you have made a mistake when God opened this door? Mistakes aren't made when you pray as fervently as we did."

But I didn't say those words. Instead I listened to Bob tell what he suspected. "Something's wrong at work. I can tell my boss is not pleased. I don't know what I'm doing wrong."

I looked out the window at my small barren backyard that wouldn't even grow grass and grieved for what I had left behind. I thought, *Why did I ever agree to pray with Bob? If I could just go back and do it over, I would be cantankerous and disagreeable. I would insist that we stay where we were.*

Here I was in a place I didn't want to be because we had prayed. The last thing I wanted to do was to continue to pray.

The next morning, though, *by habit,* I met God at my desk for a time of Bible reading, reflection, and prayer. I can't say all my grief and disappointment was resolved in those moments, but it did keep the lines of communication open. It kept me talking with God even when I didn't want to talk.

It was a good thing, too, because Bob was right in what he suspected. His boss told him, "You need to start looking for another job. Your contract will not be renewed."

Look for another job? Possibly another move. I didn't even want to think about it. I was still limp from the last move. I wasn't ready to support Bob through a job hunt or to trust God for a resolution to our dilemma.

Again the force of habit came to my rescue. Day after day, because it was my appointed time, I met God in the early morning and communed with him. During that time he never gave me a reason for what was happening, but he did help me. I was able to support Bob, continue my writing, care for our children, and teach Sunday school. Time alone with God gave me the strength and determination I needed to continue to be faithful even when I didn't understand what was happening.

The habit of praying assists us in keeping on track, but even if a person hasn't developed the habit, all is not lost. What we can't change may be God's call to us to begin praying. Now is the time to start. It may be a bit awkward at first because we are not on intimate terms with God. Nevertheless, he will help us. God is always ready to respond to his children. He wants to help us stay on the rails no matter what.

MAKING YOUR WILL MINE

What is there about what I can't change that tempts me to get off track?

How can a habitual devotional life assist me in being faithful even when I want to quit?

What steps can I take to develop the discipline of meeting God on a regular basis?

"O may I ever faithful be,
My Saviour and my God!"[9]

CHAPTER 8

WHEN GOD ANSWERS
THE PERSON

*God always answers true prayer . . . either he
changes the circumstances or supplies sufficient
power to overcome them; he answers either the
petition or the man.*[1]

HARRY EMERSON FOSDICK

The spring and summer before John went to college, he experienced a spiritual growth spurt. He earnestly and conscientiously sought God's will. As he led his church's youth group, the older members marveled at his maturity. He seemed so strong and sure of himself.

John took his Christian zeal with him to a large state university. Noticing the extensive immorality on campus, John organized a Bible study in his dorm. He was surprised by how much preparation time was required, and college itself was far more demanding than he had thought it would be. Neither had he counted on spending so much time in the lab. After three months, his Bible study dwindled to two others and himself. John felt like he was "running on empty." Home on break, he described his situation to his senior high Sunday school teacher. He said, "I wish I had someone to tell me if I am doing right. Is this how I should live as a Christian college student?"

As the teacher, Rachel, listened to John, she thought, *I'm fifteen years older than he is and I'm wishing for the same thing. These kids come and go in my Sunday school class. I keep pressing for commitment, but their attitude is "whatever." I get so exasperated; I wish I could change their nature, but I've learned I can't. I have no idea if I am making any kind of impact for Christ on their lives. After they graduate, except for a few like John, I never hear from them again.*

Both Rachel and John were unsure of their ministries. They needed reassurance.

GOD'S REASSURANCE OF JESUS

An inferred prayer of Jesus indicates that he too may have needed some reassurance. It occurred when Jesus was well into the last year of his ministry. Many followers had drifted away when they saw that Jesus was not leading them toward a Jewish superstate. Those who traveled with him hadn't caught on to who he really was after nearly three years under his teaching (Matt. 16:5-12). The opposition of the Jewish leaders had increased in intensity. Jesus was surrounded by an atmosphere of hatred. The powerful Pharisees and Sadducees wanted to destroy him (Matt. 16:1). The certainty of the cross lay ahead.

With time so short, Jesus must have wondered, *Does anyone understand me? Has anyone recognized me for who and what I am?* This was a crucial concern. William Barclay states, "His Kingdom was a kingdom within the hearts of men, and, if there was no one who had enthroned him within his heart, then his Kingdom would have ended before it ever began. But if there was someone who had recognized him and who understood him, even if as yet inadequately, then his work was safe."[2]

With his authority, Jesus could have demanded recognition from his followers. He could have repeated who he was over and over until the disciples could spit out the right answer, but that would not have reassured him. Anyone can memorize facts. Jesus needed God's reassurance, so he prayed.

ALONE, BUT NOT ALONE

Jesus withdrew from the crowds to pray, but this time he departed from his usual practice. He took his disciples with him. He took them north of Galilee to Caesarea Philippi where he could be alone with them. The Bible says, "As he was alone praying, his disciples were with him" (Luke 9:18). But why did he take the disciples this time?

* Perhaps Jesus took them with him because he wanted to set an example. He might have wanted them to connect his strength and his determination to prayer. Some time after this they would ask him, "Lord, teach us to pray" (Luke 11:1).

* Perhaps Jesus wanted the disciples there as a buffer. Their presence might have served as protection from the forces opposed to him or from the constant demands made upon him, thus enabling him to pray.

* Perhaps Jesus wanted the comfort of their companionship. One of the reasons he chose them was "that they

should be with him" (Mark 3:14a). While solitude is preferable for much of our battle with what we can't change, there will be times when we want the presence of others. They don't even have to be engaged with us in prayer. Their nearness can be comforting and supportive.

LEADING QUESTIONS

After Jesus prayed, he began asking the disciples questions. First, he asked, "Who do the crowds say I am?" Having mixed with the multitude, the disciples were aware of the various opinions about Jesus. Several answers were given.

* "John the Baptist." Here the disciples were probably quoting Herod Antipas's terrified opinion. He was scared that Jesus was a ghost sent to haunt him for murdering John the Baptist.
* "Elijah." Elijah had been taken up without dying, and Malachi said Elijah would return again.
* "Jeremiah." Before the Messiah came, some Jews thought Jeremiah would return and reveal where the ark of the covenant and the altar of incense from Solomon's temple were.
* "One of the prophets." This was a compliment. If the people regarded Jesus as a prophet, they regarded him as a man within the confidence of God (Amos 3:7).

Actually, all of the answers were intended to be compliments, but that was not what Jesus wanted or needed. Jesus pressed for a deeper answer. To those who had been with him day by day, he asked, "What about you? Who do you say I am?"

Simon Peter answered, "You are the Christ, the Son of the living God" (Matt. 16:16, NIV). Jesus exulted in Peter's answer—the Christ, the Messiah, the anointed one. Peter recognized who he was! Here was his reassurance! He said, "Blessed art thou, Simon Barjona: for flesh and blood hath not revealed it unto thee, but my Father which is in heaven" (Matt. 16:17).

In his exultation, Jesus made promises to Peter:

* I will build my church on you.
* I will give you the keys of the kingdom of heaven.
* Whatever you bind on earth shall be bound in heaven, and whatever you loose on earth shall be loosed in heaven (Matt. 16:19).

Jesus took his disciples apart for the all-important purpose of finding out if there were any who recognized him. "To his joy one man did understand, and Jesus was committing his work into the hands of that man."[3]

As joyful as Jesus was, he asked them not to tell anyone that he was the Christ (Matt. 16:20). The reassurance was for his sake; it was not an announcement to be shared with the world.

THE SUFFICIENT ANSWER

Jesus was joyful that Peter recognized him as the Christ, the Messiah, even though Peter and the other disciples did not fully comprehend what it meant. When Jesus tried to explain, Peter rebuked him (Matt. 16:22). Jesus connected being the Messiah with suffering and death. To the disciples his statements were both incredible and incomprehensible. All their lives they had thought of the Messiah in terms of irresistible conquest, and now Jesus presented ideas that staggered them. Advanced as Peter's insight was, he rejected the idea of a suffering Messiah (Matt. 16:22–23). Jesus still had work to do.

God's answer, though, was sufficient. Jesus was reassured. His close followers were beginning to perceive who he really was; he had ignited a torch in their hearts which would never go out. While the flame might have been very small at this time, it was strong enough to serve as a springboard for Jesus to teach his disciples the truth about the future.

EVERYONE WHO ASKS RECEIVES (LUKE 11:10a)

We can learn some helpful things from Jesus' prayer for reassurance and the answer he received. If we take these lessons to heart, they can eliminate a lot of frustration from our praying and from the answers we receive about what we can't change.

1. *God doesn't always answer directly.* God answers us in a variety of ways. Often it is that "Abba, Father" type of assurance—an inner witness of the Holy Spirit. Other times he answers by giving us tools to find what we are seeking. When Jesus prayed for reassurance, God responded by giving him a tool—questions to use. When Jesus used those questions, God gave him the answer he needed.

When John returned to campus, he continued to be

haunted by his need to know if he were correctly living the Christian life. Urgently and passionately, he prayed about it. The next morning on the way to the cafeteria, the thought came to him that he ought to talk with Dr. Miller, John's major professor and one of the few Christian faculty members on campus.

When John told Dr. Miller about his concern, Dr. Miller responded, "John, I've noticed your struggle to try to keep up with your studies, your lab hours, and also prepare for the Bible studies. You are trying to do too much. I advise you to concentrate on your studies so that you can be a well-trained person to lead Bible studies *after* college. This doesn't mean you should let up in your moral stand or in your devotional life, but do give up the Bible study. You are not a strong enough student to handle it all."

With a clarity that John hadn't had before, he saw his personal limitations. A peace welled up in his heart as he recognized God's answer in Dr. Miller's words. He now knew what to do.

2. *God's answer may not be perfect in the sense that we will no longer have any struggle with what we can't change.* When Jesus chose the Twelve (chap. 6), God's answer was not perfect. One of them eventually denied Jesus, and another one betrayed him to his enemies. When he needed reassurance, it was given through Peter, but Jesus still had to educate the apostles about who he was. It wasn't until the resurrection that the disciples finally understood what being the Messiah really meant.

Our struggle with unchangeables may not be eliminated by one swooping answer to prayer. God will answer our prayer, but his answer doesn't necessarily mean *end of struggle.*

It was the end of struggle that Rachel wanted. She longed for the day when there would be no struggle in working with high school students. She kept thinking that if she became good enough as a Sunday school teacher, the struggle would cease. Her class would be perfect, and she would see marvelous results.

Isn't that what many of us want? We want to finally graduate from the school of hard knocks to a post-graduate plain, free from the stress of relationships and challenging growth. Unconsciously, we sometimes pray with this perfect vision in mind.

God's answers, though, may not be perfect in the sense that struggle is eliminated. His answers may be part of a process for some purpose he wants to achieve in our life. Jesus was being made fully adequate for his destined work (Heb. 2:10). He was learning obedience by the things which he suffered (Heb. 5:8). He was tempted like we are (Heb. 4:15) and was made like his brothers and sisters so he might be a merciful and faithful high priest (Heb. 2:17).

Because we know the outcome in Jesus' life, it would be easy to lose sight of the fact that a process was involved. It's also easy to lose sight of the same possibility in our own life. We may want the perfect answer so much that we fail to see that God might be molding and shaping us into some person we never dreamed about being, or achieving some purpose we never considered.

3. *Even when God's answer involves struggle, it will be sufficient.* The men Jesus chose to be his apostles changed the world. Peter's answer gave Jesus the reassurance he needed.

In both instances—and in instances to come—God gave Jesus what he needed to carry on, even though he did not take away the cross or its accompanying struggles. God's answers were sufficient to meet Jesus' needs.

That God's answer will be sufficient is a great consolation. The answer may not be specifically what we asked for, but it will meet our needs.

This truth explains an amazing statement that Adoniram Judson made at the close of his life. This renowned American missionary of the early 1800s said, "I never prayed sincerely and earnestly for anything, but it came; at some time—no matter at how distant a day—somehow, in some shape—probably the last I should have devised—it came." But Judson had prayed for entrance into India and had been compelled to go to Burma; he had prayed for his wife's life, and had buried both her and his two children; he had prayed for release from the king of Ava's prison and had lain there months, chained and miserable. Scores of Judson's petitions had gone without an affirmative answer. But *Judson* always had been answered. He had been upheld, guided, reinforced; unforeseen doors had opened through the very trials he sought to avoid; and the deep desires of his life were being accomplished not in his way but beyond his way.[4]

As we have seen and will continue to see, Jesus brought his needs regarding his destiny to God through prayer. God's answers did not always mean the end of struggle, but they were sufficient. *God always answered Jesus,* and that's what we can rely on. God will always answer *us.*

MAKING YOUR WILL MINE

What mental image do I have of the answer
I want from God?

What is the difference between a sufficient answer and a perfect answer? Am I willing to trust God for the sufficent answer?

Beyond meeting my immediate need with his answer, what greater purpose may God have in mind?

"I pray that the God of peace will give me every good thing I need so that I can do what he wants. . . . I pray that God, through Christ, will do in me what pleases him."[5]

CHAPTER 9

NEEDED: A GLIMPSE OF GLORY

When your burden becomes too heavy, when life's
ways become too dark, when the heart is too sore,
when you are ready to perish, it is not amiss to
pray to God to open the heavens, and through a
rift in the sky to shine down into your heart some
of the light of the Glory World.[1]

B. H. CARROLL

After Peter's confession of "Thou art the Christ," Jesus began revealing in plain, matter-of-fact statements what lay ahead:

* "I must go to Jerusalem" (see Matt. 16:21).
* "I must suffer many things at the hands of the elders, chief priests, and scribes" (see Matt. 16:21; Mark 8:31; and Luke 9:22).
* "I will be killed" (see Matt. 16:21).

Jesus attempted to relieve the dark message of death by the bright hope of the resurrection. He said, "But three days later I will be raised to life" (Matt. 16:21d, TEV). His disciples were too shocked by Jesus' words about death and enemies to hear the words of hope. A suffering Messiah was entirely foreign to their way of thinking. He was to be a conqueror, not one to die at the hands of his enemies.

Surely they thought, *He has taken too gloomy a view of the united opposition of the Pharisees and Sadducees.* "They found a ready spokesman of their thoughts and feelings in Peter, who had but now received such a warm expression of approval from Jesus for His whole-hearted confession."[2] Peter took Jesus aside and began to rebuke him: "God forbid it, Lord! . . . That must never happen to you!" (Matt. 16:22b, TEV).

Now Jesus must have been the one surprised. "Jesus turned around and said to Peter, 'Get away from me, Satan! You are an obstacle in my way, because these thoughts of yours don't come from God, but from man' " (Matt. 16:23, TEV).

Why did Jesus issue this stinging rebuke?

* Perhaps Jesus was grieved that Peter—the one who had made such a noble confession of faith—didn't have a fuller grasp of what being the Messiah meant. Many teachers have moments of discouragement when they wonder, Aren't my students ever going to catch on? All through Jesus' ministry there had been half-veiled intimations about the necessity of his dying,[3] but none of these symbolic references had been fully understood by the twelve apostles.

* Since Jesus called Peter "Satan," he may have seen Peter's concern as tempting him to get off course the way Satan had tried to tempt him in the wilderness. This time, though, the temptation came from one Jesus loved and praised. That made it harder to resist, which may be why he responded so decisively.

* When Jesus spoke the words out loud about his suffering and death, perhaps he was reminded of the reality of what was ahead.[4] To be human is to struggle with death. By his strong answer, perhaps Jesus was saying, "This is awful enough as it is, Peter. Don't tempt me by suggesting there is a way out."

Jesus didn't try to soften his retort; instead, he proceeded to teach what following him meant:

* Deny yourself (Matt. 16:24).
* Take up your cross (Matt. 16:24).
* Lose your life to save it (Matt. 16:25).
* Forfeit the world's gain to save your soul (Matt. 16:26).

You can almost hear his listeners gasp, "This teaching is too hard." Peter must have thought words that he said on another occasion, "Look, we have left everything to follow you" (see Matt. 19:27).

Trying to teach the disciples what the Messiah was like and what true followship meant must have been discouraging for Jesus. About a week after he began his hard, clear teaching, Jesus withdrew to a mountain (Luke 9:28). According to Curtis C. Mitchell, "The grammar makes it crystal clear that the avowed purpose of the excursion was for prayer."[5]

ON THE MOUNTAINTOP

Jesus took Peter, John and James with him. They were the "three disciples most capable of understanding him and entering with him into a consideration of his death."[6]

The prayer session must have been long because Peter,

James, and John, weary after the day's work and the ascent of the mountain, soon fell asleep. While they slept, Jesus prayed.

While he was praying, his countenance was altered (Luke 9:29). His garments "became shining, exceeding white as snow" (Mark 9:3) and "dazzling" (Luke 9:29, TLB).

Roused by the splendor, the disciples woke up. When they were wide awake, they saw his glory. They also saw Moses and Elijah talking with Jesus. This sparked a conversation between Peter and Jesus. While they were talking, a cloud appeared and covered them with its shadow. God's voice from the cloud said, "This is my Son, whom I have chosen; listen to him" (Luke 9:35, NIV).

JESUS' TRANSFIGURATION

This event gives us a graphic picture of how God encouraged Jesus. "Every line of the picture portrays God's visitation."[7]

The change in countenance. As Jesus prayed, an inner change took place. The first outward evidence that God was renewing his strength was a change in his countenance. "His face did shine as the sun" (Matt. 17:2b).

The change in raiment. "There was a kind of effulgence—a celestial radiance—shining out over all. The Divinity within broke through the veil of the flesh and shone out, until His very raiment kindled to the dazzling brightness of the light."[8]

The appearance of Moses and Elijah. Here were two supreme figures among Jews: Moses was the supreme lawgiver, and Elijah was the supreme prophet. Their appearance encouraged Jesus. "It is as if they said to him: 'It is you who are right, and it is the popular teachers who are wrong;

it is you in whom there is the fulfilment of all that the law says and all that the prophets foretold. The real fulfilment of the past is not in the popular idea of might and power, but in your way of sacrificial love.' "[9]

Moses' and Elijah's conversation with Jesus. They spoke about the way Jesus would fulfill God's purpose by dying in Jerusalem (Luke 9:31). What two better people to talk to Jesus about dying than Moses and Elijah? They were representative of those who witnessed and suffered for God, and for whom the end was not tragedy but triumph. The encouragement for Jesus was that if he went on, there would certainly be a cross, but there would equally certainly be the glory.[10]

The cloud that appeared. This cloud is thought to be the *shechinah* glory of God. All through the history of Israel there was the idea of the *shechinah,* the glory of God. Again and again this glory appeared to the people in the form of a cloud. Now the glory of God was upon Jesus, assuring him of God's approval on what he was doing.

God's audible words. In the Greek, God's words go something like this: "This is my Son, the dearly-beloved one; be constantly hearing him." God was confirming the rightness of Jesus' interpretation of himself and of what it means to follow him.

"For Jesus the transfiguration brought new strength . . . and added patience, through a foretaste of the glory He should experience after His passion."[11]

ENCOURAGEMENT FOR THE DISCIPLES

When Peter, James, and John saw Jesus' shining face and his glistening garments, they were "eyewitnesses of his majesty" (2 Pet. 1:16). No Jew would have seen that luminous cloud without thinking of the glory of God resting upon his people. Surely here was something which would lift up the hearts of the disciples. Here was something that would enable them to see the glory beyond the shame and humiliation. They still did not fully understand, but the transfiguration must surely have given them some little glimmering that the future was not all grim.

When the disciples heard God's voice, they fell on their faces in awe and were afraid. Ray Summers, in his *Commentary on Luke,* describes the significance of this event:

> *This is my Son* indicates that the voice spoke to the three disciples and for their benefit. In the baptism experience the same phrase had been used (from Psalm 2:7), but it was directed to Jesus . . . At the baptism, the voice said to Jesus, "You are my Son"; at the transfiguration it said to the disciples, "This is my Son."
>
> *Listen to him:* The tense of the imperative indicates continuous action—"keep on listening to him." The chain of events starting with Peter's confession indicates that the command to listen referred to their listening to what Jesus was saying about his death. They had confessed faith that Jesus was the Son of God, and now the voice from heaven—right out of the cloud of God's presence—confirmed that confession. . . . The voice from heaven was saying essentially, "Keep on listening to what he is saying about the necessity of his death."[12]

ENCOURAGEMENT FOR US

God's encouragement to Jesus, Peter, James, and John in response to Jesus' praying should encourage us to pray when we are discouraged. B. H. Carroll describes these times of discouragement in his book *Messages on Prayer:*

> There are parts of the path of our earthly pilgrimage full of thorns and leading up steep declivities; parts of the way are overshadowed by clouds reaching down into the very valley of the shadow of death. Sometimes we are called upon to bear things that are almost unbearable, and to do things, in the weakness of the flesh, almost impossible; sometimes we sorely hunger for the viands of the heavenly banquet, and crave with intense longing the joys of everlasting and final deliverance.[13]

It is not wrong at such times to ask for a glimpse of glory. Though the Holy Spirit is given to us as a pledge of all God will ultimately bestow on us, we still sometimes need a partial glimpse, some transfiguration experience here on earth, to enable us to carry on.

* When we feel suffocated by the thought of our own death, we can pray, "God, reassure me there is life after death."
* When we are bogged down in grief over the death of a loved one, we can pray, "Show me in some way that I will see her again."
* When our mirror and our energy remind us that we are getting older, we can pray, "Father, show me I will always have significance in your kingdom."
* When we lie awake nights wistfully contemplating "what might have been," we can ask God for a vision for the future.
* When we grow discouraged living the holy life, when we've witnessed and taught with no visible

response, we can cry out, "God, if you are real, show me yourself all over again."

Constant discouragement about what we can't change can make us lose all self-confidence and our enthusiasm for living. We can conclude that it is simply not worth trying any more. This is when it is time to ask God for a glimpse of glory. Through prayer we can be spiritually transformed to handle what we can't change. This is when "we are most likely to witness, in whatever measure may be possible for us, the glory of God."[14]

A SMALL GLIMPSE WILL DO

Our glimpse of glory doesn't have to be spectacular like Jesus' transfiguration. A small rift in the sky to let God's glory shine through may be just enough to keep us from giving up. It was for my friend Jan and her daughter Andrea.

Andrea was almost killed in a terrible accident while serving as a foreign missionary. Afterwards she had to return to the United States because she suffered from post traumatic stress syndrome. It was a discouraging time for Andrea and her whole family.

Although the doctor for Andrea's missionary organization was located about three hours away from Jan's home, Jan said she never minded taking Andrea to the doctor. In addition to being medically well qualified, the doctor was a good counselor. She was always able to get Andrea to talk, something the family couldn't do. She and Andrea always prayed together before the session ended.

When Jan dropped Andrea off, she would watch her walk to the door of the doctor's office. Her shoulders were slumped, she drug her feet, her eyes were listless, and her face had a grayish tone.

When Andrea came out of the doctor's office, she was smiling, the gray color was gone, and her steps were certain and deliberate. Jan said, "Seeing the change in Andrea was always worth the time and inconvenience of traveling to the doctor. Once Andrea talked and prayed with the doctor, she was encouraged. Her renewed hope was reflected in her appearance. When she had hope, our whole family was encouraged."

One visit with the doctor was not enough to cure Andrea; the healing process was a long one. Yet each individual visit was enough to encourage Andrea and her family. Each visit enabled them to carry on.

When the Glimpse Is Spectacular

Occasionally, God's encouragement in response to our praying may be spectacular, at least to us. The nature of the experience may be so unusual or dramatic that we may be tempted to magnify it like Peter did. He wanted to prepare three booths, linger on the mountain, and not come down again (Matt. 17:4; Mark 9:5; Luke 9:33). He wanted to prolong the great moment and not return to the everyday world. Likewise, we may want to focus on God's encouragement so much that we lose sight of why God gave it to us.

Or, the relief we experience—whether the glimpse of glory is small or spectacular—may be misleading. We may assume that our struggle with what we can't change is over when it isn't.

Our glimpse of glory is to be a temporary support. It is to give us strength to keep walking. Experiencing the glory of God did not prompt Jesus to remain on the mountain. It put him right back on the path he had been walking—the path toward the cross.

MAKING YOUR WILL MINE

What does it mean to be spiritually transfigured?

When should I seek a glimpse of glory?

How may I open myself to a transfiguration experience?

"Almighty Father,
whose Son was revealed in majesty
before he suffered death upon the cross:
give us faith to perceive his glory,
that we may be strengthened to suffer with him
and be changed into his likeness, from glory to
glory."[15]

CHAPTER 10

"FOR SO IT SEEMED GOOD . . ."

*Praise is the highest form of faith; for when we
cannot see the answer and yet praise, we are
telling God that we trust Him, love Him, and dare
leave the final and ultimate answer to Him.[1]*

JOHN P. NEWPORT

Finding a job in higher education is very difficult because the field is saturated. By the time my husband's university contract had ended (see chap. 7), he had had only two job interviews. A local Bible training school had an opening, but Bob had put off inquiring because the school was not accredited. With no work and no job in sight, Bob applied. The Bible training school hired him as registrar and teacher—a job he liked very much.

Since Bob wouldn't have worked for a non-accredited school before, since he was happy in his new job, since he could make a significant contribution to God's kingdom at a Bible training school, I concluded that this job was what God had originally intended for Bob. The job with the major university was God's way of getting us to the area where the training school was located.

I was so confident of my interpretation that I suggested to Bob that we needed a better place to raise our sons. At the time we were living in a crowded neighborhood with small fenced backyards, even smaller front yards, and cars lining the street. There was no place for growing boys to explore and to play ball.

We bought a house in the country. With a pond beside it, a big yard, and lots of trees, the house provided an idyllic setting for raising boys. In fact, years later, when our oldest son was in college, he wrote a paper about it and called it "The Dreamstead."

When we had been in our new home one year, I was ready to celebrate. I made a cake and planned to serve it—with one candle in the middle—for dinner. I relaxed with the boys in the afternoon. We were outside playing when Bob arrived home.

As the station wagon pulled up, I noticed the back end was filled with books. Looking closer, I saw they were Bob's books.

"Why are you bringing your books home?"

Bob answered, "I've been fired."

His words were like a powerful explosion that blasted away my inner strength. I leaned against the car for support and asked, "What happened?"

"The boss called me into his office about three o'clock. He told me the school wouldn't be needing me anymore, to clean out my office, and then he handed me my severance pay. He never gave me a reason."

Our evening meal was quiet. The celebration candle

forgotten. Afterwards, I worked in the yard. I knew Bob needed me, but I wanted to be alone with my thoughts. *What would we do? Who would ever hire someone who had been fired so close together? Would we have to move? Leave our country home?* In between the questions, a refrain played itself over and over, "I can't go through it again." The anxiousness, the uncertainty, and the stress of the first job loss were still fresh in my memory.

Most people can handle major stresses (like being fired) if they occur several years apart. (Ten years apart is good!) I wasn't emotionally or spiritually ready to support Bob, although practically we managed. To stretch his severance pay as far as possible, Bob took a temporary, minimum-wage job at a window factory while he looked for another job in higher education. I started baby-sitting a neighbor's child after school to add to my writing income.

In the afternoons, when Bob arrived home from the window factory and the older children arrived home from school, I fixed hot tea and snacks. Once the children left the table, Bob and I lingered to sip tea and talk. A lot of our talk centered on trying to figure out why Bob had been fired. When the conversation turned to the future, we grew quiet, and a feeling of hopelessness descended on us.

It's not unusual to feel fragile and hopeless when hit by shocking news. News that jars your life may come via the telephone. You pick up the receiver expecting a friend's call or a telephone solicitor and you hear words that forever alter your life. Or, the news may come by a knock on the door. When you open it, a policeman stands there. He says, "I'm sorry to have to tell you, but there's been an accident, a serious accident. Your daughter (or father or spouse) was injured." The jolting news leaves you feeling weak and highly vulnerable.

Bob and I felt like two toothpicks trying to hold each other up. We needed to lean on the other, but neither of us had much strength to offer back. In the past, I would have tried to encourage Bob. I would have expressed confidence in him, in God, and in the future; but I didn't see much of a future for us.

With little hope, I did what I had already learned to do, and that was to "stay on the rails no matter what." Albeit limply, I stuck to my schedule of early morning devotional time, getting Bob off to work and the older children off to school, caring for our youngest at home, researching and writing during the mornings, and doing housework and errands in the early afternoons. In the routine of staying committed, I discovered a key that reduced my fragility, ignited hope, and changed my perspective.

As it happened, my writing project at the time was the prayer life of Jesus. My assignment was to find patterns in his prayer life, report them, and show how to apply them. His pattern of frequent withdrawals was easy to spot. As I looked closer, I spotted a second pattern.

A PATTERN OF THANKSGIVING

Jesus' prayer life incorporated a pattern of thanksgiving. Scripture provides numerous examples of situations where Jesus responded with thanksgiving.

* *When resources were limited.* When the crowd of five thousand men plus women and children gathered to be near Jesus and to experience his healing power, they stayed until it was time to eat. Jesus wanted to feed them. The disciples insisted they didn't have enough food. " 'All we have here are five loaves and two fish,' they replied" (Matt. 14:17, TEV). Did Jesus change his desire in light of the limited re-

sources? No, he organized the crowd, took the five loaves and two fish, looked up to heaven, and gave thanks. He then told the disciples to pass the food around; there was more than enough for everyone.

On another occasion (Matt. 15:32–39; Mark 8:1–10), Jesus did the same thing with seven loaves and a few small fish when four thousand men, plus women and children, needed feeding.

* *When people were unbelieving.* Jesus offered precious miracles to the people living in the towns of Chorazin, Bethsaida, and Capernaum (Matt. 11:20–24), and they completely disregarded them. How did Jesus react to this kind of treatment? He pronounced woes upon them, and then surprisingly, he offered thanks: "I thank thee, O Father, Lord of heaven and earth, because thou hast hid these things from the wise and prudent, and hast revealed them unto babes. Even so, Father: for so it seemed good in thy sight" (Matt. 11:25–26).

* *When the seventy returned.* The seventy were followers of Jesus whom he had sent out in twos to go ahead of him to every place where he himself was about to go. The seventy found, apparently to their surprise, that people did listen and that healings actually occurred. "Lord," they said, "even the devils are subject unto us through thy name" (Luke 10:17). Jesus rejoiced in spirit and offered the same prayer he said for those who disregarded his miracles. He said, "I thank thee, O Father, Lord of heaven and earth, that thou hast hid these things from the wise and prudent, and hast revealed them unto babes: even so, Father; for so it seemed good in thy sight" (Luke 10:21).

* *At the tomb of a friend.* When Jesus received word that his friend, Lazarus, was ill, he returned to Bethany from Perea. By the time he arrived, Lazarus was dead. Mourners

had gathered. Emotion was running high. Jesus wept with Lazarus's sisters, Mary and Martha. Before saying the word of power that would bring Lazarus out of the grave (before the miracle ever occurred), Jesus lifted up his eyes to heaven and said, "Father, I thank thee that thou hast heard me. And I knew that thou hearest me always" (John 11:41b–42a). Clearly, Jesus had already prayed for Lazarus to be raised from the dead. In this prayer at the tomb, in front of the gathered crowd and before the actual evidence of the resurrection, Jesus thanked God.

* *When the disciples were irritated.* One day in the midst of a crowd, some little children were clamoring to get closer to Jesus. In the judgment of the disciples, Jesus had more important people to see, so they shooed the children away. When Jesus saw what was happening, he said, "Suffer the little children to come unto me, and forbid them not" (Mark 10:14). Then Jesus took them in his arms and blessed them (Mark 10:16).

* *When the end was near.* The most solemn prayer of thanksgiving Jesus offered was when he sat down with the Twelve to keep the last Passover meal. With profound emotion Jesus "took the cup, and gave thanks" (Matt. 26:27). The fact that he was instituting a way of remembrance for us doesn't take away from the emotion it cost him at the time. As Jesus gave thanks, he was on his way to the cross; he was in the process of being betrayed; and he was about to be deserted by some of his closest friends.

* *When sharing a meal.* When two discouraged disciples met the resurrected Jesus on the road to Emmaus, they did not know him. After chatting with him for a while, they invited Jesus to share a meal with them (Luke 24:30–31). During the blessing and as the food was passed around the table, the eyes of the two disciples were opened. They rec-

ognized him when he sat down with them, picked up a simple loaf of bread, blessed it, and broke it. Remembering other times of thanksgiving—the breaking of five small loaves, the handling of small children, the passing of a cup of wine—they recognized the stranger in their midst.

Gratitude was an integral part of Jesus' prayer life, whether he was walking in the light or in the shadow. Thanksgiving leaped to his lips, not just in life's shining hours, but also during difficult times. I marveled at his ability to praise God in the dark hours, but I couldn't bring myself to say, "Thank you, Father, that Bob lost his job." I wasn't thankful, and I didn't expect to ever be thankful.

A LITTLE GRATITUDE GOES A LONG WAY

I had made it a practice, though, not to recommend spiritual principles to my readers unless I was willing to practice them. After pulling together the facts of Jesus' pattern of gratitude, it was time to think about application. I had no problem recommending thanksgiving for the good times, but how could I counsel my readers to practice it when times were bleak if I wasn't willing to do it?

As I polished the manuscript, typing and retyping the facts, I was drawn to the phrase, "for so it seemed good in thy sight." It comes from the prayer Jesus prayed on a joyful occasion *and* during a difficult time. These words show that the main characteristic of Jesus' life was obedience to his Father's will. "They bear eloquent testimony to the truth that whatever the Father's gracious will might be, it was accepted without question by His Son, even if, humanly speaking, acceptance might involve him in much disappointment and distress."[2]

If Jesus could pray those words when his miracles were rejected, perhaps I could at least try saying them. I printed "for so it seemed good in thy sight" on a three-by-five card and placed it at the base of the desk lamp. I repeated the words in my morning prayers. Throughout the morning, I spoke the words out loud when I happened to glance toward the card. I whispered them when I hung clothes on the line and when I walked to the mailbox.

Slowly, praying those words made a difference—not a large difference but a significant difference. They ignited just enough hope to change my perspective. Perhaps in some deep, mysterious way God was accomplishing something in our lives that I couldn't begin to fathom or understand.

With that little bit of hope, my inner strength began to return and my feelings of fragility lessened. I stopped saying, "I can't go through it again."

I was now able to encourage Bob. Our afternoon tea times became planning sessions as Bob and I stopped talking about the past and dreamed again of possibilities for the future. Gratitude made the difference.

MAKING YOUR WILL MINE

If I cannot thank God for what I cannot change, is there one thing within my situation that I can thank him for?

If I am skeptical about the power of gratitude, am I still willing to begin every one of my prayers in the next two weeks with words of thanks?

If I am at a loss for words, am I willing to pray the words
of a biblical "pray-er" such as
* Hagar—"Thou God seest me" (Gen. 16:13).
* Jeremiah—"Great are your purposes and
mighty are your deeds" (Jer. 32:19a, NIV).
* Habakkuk—"Yet I will rejoice in the Lord"
(Hab. 3:18a, NIV).
* Jesus—"Even so, Father; for so it seemed
good in thy sight" (Matt. 11:26).

How would I benefit if I find something to be thankful for
regarding what I cannot change?

How can I make thanksgiving an integral part of my
prayer life?

*"Yet I will rejoice. . . . Father; for so it seemed good
in thy sight."*[3]

CHAPTER 11

"NOW MY HEART IS TROUBLED . . ."

"I have come to bring fire to the earth, and, oh, that my task was completed! There is a terrible baptism ahead of me, and how I am pent up until it is accomplished!"

JESUS, LUKE 12:49–50, TLB

Sometimes in a movie, the pace picks up and scenes flash quickly, one after the other, on the screen. This technique may be used to save time; many years of history can be covered quickly. It can also create an emotional climate that will help us understand what a character is going to say or do.

We need to use this technique of flashing scenes[1] to understand Jesus when he said, "Now my heart is troubled" (John 12:27a, TEV). This is not something we would expect a regular and grateful "pray-er" to say. So, what prompted this statement?

A QUICK LOOK

Scene: Jesus is standing in front of a tomb. The people gathered around are weeping. In a loud voice, Jesus says, "Lazarus come forth."

Scene: Pharisees and chief priests address the Sanhedrin (John 11:45–53). One Pharisee says, "What shall we do? Look at all the miracles this man Jesus is performing!" Another Pharisee says, "If we let him go on this way, everyone will believe in him, and the Roman authorities will destroy our temple and nation?"

A chief priest responds, "We can't let that happen. We have to get rid of him."

Scene: Jesus and his disciples are walking toward a desert. The gate of Jerusalem is behind them. A disciple says to Jesus, "I don't understand why we are leaving. You had more followers than ever after you brought Lazarus back to life. What you did was awesome."

Scene: The streets of Jerusalem are filled with people mingling and talking (John 11:55–57). One person asks, "What do you think? Will Jesus come to town for Passover?"

Another answers, "Surely not. He won't show his face around here. He's a wanted man. Remember, if we see him we are supposed to report it to the Pharisees and chief priests. They will see that he is arrested."

Another person says, "I believe he has the courage to return to Jerusalem; but if he's smart, he'll stay away."

Scene: A resident of Jerusalem says, "Have you heard? Jesus is in Bethany."

"No, you're kidding!" exclaims another.

"Let's go there. It's an easy walk."

"I'm for it. I want to see Jesus; I've heard so much about him."

"Lazarus is who I want to see. Imagine coming back to life after four days in the tomb!"

Scene: Many people are exiting Jerusalem. A Pharisee in the group turns to another Pharisee and says, "Let's get the Sanhedrin together. I can see we're going to have to get rid of Lazarus in addition to Jesus. Too many of our followers are interested in Jesus because of the miracle of Lazarus" (see John 12:11).

Scene: The streets of Jerusalem are lined with people. Jesus rides into Jerusalem on a donkey. The people shout, "Praise God! God bless him who comes in the name of the Lord!" The people spread their cloaks on the road, and they wave palm branches.

Scene: Gazing over Jerusalem, Jesus weeps, "If you only knew what is needed for peace! I ride into town on a donkey so you can see I am on a peaceful mission. If I had chosen a horse, then I might have been representing myself as the warrior you want. O Jerusalem, will you ever understand?"

Scene: At the temple in Jerusalem, Jesus heals the blind and lame (Matt. 21:14). Little children sing, "Hosanna to the Son of David" (Matt. 21:15). Jewish authorities watch. Their arms are crossed; their faces are scowling; their eyes are livid with anger (Matt. 21:15).

Scene: Jesus knocks over the tables of the money changers and the stalls of those selling sacrificial animals in the temple. As he drives out the merchants and their customers, he says, "The Scriptures declare, 'My temple will be called a place of prayer,' but you have turned it into a den of thieves!" (Matt. 21:13, NLT).

Scene: Philip and Andrew tell Jesus, "Some Greeks are in town for the Passover. They want to see you." Jesus answers, "The hour has now come for the Son of man to receive great glory" (John 12:23, TEV).

It was at this point, after the request of the Greeks, that Jesus admitted to having a troubled heart (John 12:27a).

THE DISTURBING STRANDS

By looking at the scenes, we can see various threads that intermingle, overlap, and tangle to give Jesus a troubled heart.

The determined opposition. Wherever he was, whatever he was doing, the Jewish authorities were watching, criticizing, and scheming. They were incessant.

The ever-present crowd. Everywhere Jesus went, people followed. He was a curiosity attraction, a phenomenal miracle-worker, a daring temple-cleanser. Weren't the people ever going to understand his mission and his nature?

His approaching death. Previously, Jesus had spoken of his "hour" (John 2:4; 7:6; 7:30; 8:20). Each time, he indicated that it had not yet come. He had also said that he would lay down his life (John 10:11, 15) and that other sheep not belonging to the fold (the Gentiles) would join his flock (John 10:16). The request of the Greeks was a signal that it was time for that to happen. To bring them in required his death (John 12:24).

It was one thing to talk about death; it was another to be the life that gives itself. Jesus admitted he was "troubled," a word that means "deeply agitated."[2]

FROM TENSION TO TRIUMPH

At that moment, Jesus must have wanted to withdraw from the crowd. He must have longed for the relief and refreshment he had found in lonely places on other occasions. But he was not alone. He was surrounded by people (John 12:29). Not being able to escape, Jesus did the next best thing. He prayed where he was: "Now is my soul troubled; and what shall I say? Father, save me from this hour: but for this cause came I unto this hour. Father, glorify thy name" (John 12:27–28a).

Immediately an answer came. A voice from heaven said, "I have both glorified it, and will glorify it again" (John 12:28). God had been glorified by the work of Jesus in the past, and he would be glorified in the future. The crowd standing around heard the voice but were unable to distinguish what was said. Some said it was thunder, while others said an angel spoke to Jesus (John 12:29).

The voice, Jesus said, was for the people (John 12:30). However, as dramatic as a voice from heaven might be, it made no significant change in the people at the time. They went right on misunderstanding (John 12:34). Jesus was the one who was helped by his prayer.

"Fortified by an overwhelming sense of heavenly approval, Jesus triumphantly cried, 'Now . . . is the judgment of this world.' "[3] Confidently he told them, "When I am lifted up from the earth, I will draw everyone to me" (John 12:32, TEV). The relief gained from the prayer served to steel Jesus' determination to continue toward the cross.

A PRESCRIPTION FOR TROUBLED HEARTS

It is not unusual to experience a troubled heart when we are dealing with what we can't change. We may be so perplexed by God's actions in our lives that we want to pull away from him. At the same time, we long for the peace that only he can give. We may be wanting our will to be done, and yet, we know our desire ought to be the same as

Jesus', to glorify God's name. Until we've adjusted to what we can't change, we may want to withdraw from life, but we can't. There are ever-present jobs, deadlines, children, and relationships. The stress bears in on us, adding to the weight of our perplexity.

Jesus' prescription for troubled hearts is honest praying. Right in the middle of people who did not fully understand him and, therefore, were not sympathetic to his needs, Jesus confessed his troubled state and wondered what to do.

Some say Jesus' feelings and thoughts were not a part of his prayer. Bible translators and commentators disagree over exactly what was his prayer. Some say all of John 12:27–28a, beginning with "Now is my soul troubled . . ." and ending with ". . . glorify thy name," was his prayer. Others say his prayer was simply "Father, glorify thy name."[4]

If all the passage was Jesus' prayer, then Jesus honestly expressed his feelings and thoughts in prayer. He did not suffer in silence and hold back what he was experiencing as if he had to present some kind of "dressed-up, formal" version of himself to God.

If Jesus' prayer was simply, "Father, glorify thy name," then he must have felt free to confess to others. He said how he felt and then wondered out loud, "Should I pray for escape or should I go on?"[5] He reminded himself of what he had known for a long time—that he came into the world for this moment—and then he prayed.

Either way, honesty and prayer are linked. Whether Jesus honestly confessed to others and then prayed or whether his confession was wrapped up in his prayer to God, he let us know that it is all right to express our thoughts and feelings.

Honesty with God

Throughout the years of studying and preparing for a career in higher education, my husband had a continuing love for preaching. In fact, Bob had taught preaching at the Bible training center where he had been registrar. As we sipped tea in the afternoons when he came home from the window factory, we talked about his skills, his strengths, and his desire to serve the Lord. We wondered if God was using the job losses to channel his love for preaching into a full-time ministry. We talked with our pastor about it, and he, too, seemed to feel this was the case. He advised Bob to make a public commitment to the ministry before our church, and Bob did.

That widened the job possibilities for Bob, but none was forthcoming even though he wrote many letters and made many contacts. Eventually Bob had to quit the window factory job because it only paid minimum wage. He became an executive recruiter to support our family.

Meanwhile, the dream lingered for a job in higher education, but the months turned into years. As Bob recalls it, "I was getting further and further away from what I felt called to do. It was like I was standing on a train platform. The train was going by, and I could see the caboose."

Then a severe recession hit our area. Companies stopped hiring; "head-hunter" services were no longer needed.

Bob said, "Were the promises of God applicable to everyone but me? One of my favorite promises was, 'Trust in the LORD with all thine heart; and lean not unto thine own understanding. In all thy ways acknowledge him, and he shall direct thy paths' (Prov. 3:5–6). If God was directing my path—where was it?"

Reading the parable of the talents (Matt. 25:14–30) prompted Bob to be honest about his perplexing situation. This parable implies that we will be held accountable for how we use our gifts and abilities, so Bob prayed, "God, I have done everything I know to get a job in a school or a church. If you cannot perform, intervene, or act on my behalf in some way, then when I stand before you on judgment day, I don't want to hear you say, 'Bob, you were not a good steward of the time and talents I gave you.' When you ask me what I have done with my life, I will not be disrespectful, but I will say, 'You explain it, I can't.' I cannot be held accountable for not being given an opportunity to use my talents."

After Bob honestly prayed, nothing outwardly changed, but inwardly everything did. The inner tension that he had been carrying around with him disappeared. He felt at peace with himself and God. Afterwards, he said, "The responsibility for what I did with my life was no longer solely mine. If God had called me—and I believed he had—then he shared in the responsibility of what I did with my life."

Honesty with Others

Some would rather confess their troubled hearts to others than directly to God. When we do so, we don't have to give a complete case history of our tension or trace all its details. In a Wednesday night prayer meeting, in a Sunday school class, in a Bible study, or among close friends, we might say, "I'm struggling with something I can't change. The tension inside is so great I can't seem to sort out what I'm feeling. I want to do right, but I'm having trouble knowing what that is. I need you to pray with me."

Honest confession breaks up the swirling emotions and

thoughts that trouble our hearts. Verbalizing the tension we are experiencing diminishes its power, freeing us to pray as we ought, "Father, glorify thy name."

When our hearts are troubled about what we can't change, it's time to be honest, and it's time to pray. When we do, we give God a clear channel to respond to us. He will relieve our tension-filled hearts and strengthen us to handle what we cannot change.

MAKING YOUR WILL MINE

What is troubling me about what I can't change?

What additional concerns and responsibilities do I have that increase my tension?

How will honest praying, either alone or with others, help me?

"The troubles of my heart are enlarged: O bring thou me out of my distresses."[6]

CHAPTER 12

BUT I HAVE PRAYED FOR YOU

*We often find ourselves in a wilderness overrun
with hazards which threaten to overwhelm us. It is
then that we must remember . . . and be
strengthened by the fact that Yeshua, our High
Priest, is faithfully praying for us.*[1]

STUART SACKS

When Greg's (from chap. 1) manager told him he didn't
have what it took for a professional baseball career, his first
thoughts were, *I'll show him. One way or the other, I'm going
to be a professional baseball player.*

His second thoughts were of his family. Greg and Cindy
had married while college students, right before their junior
year. After graduation and while confident of his future,
they started planning a family. Cindy was now six months
pregnant. *Would the energy and time involved in trying to
stay in baseball be fair to her and to their child?*

While trying to decide what to do, Greg had moments

in which he wished he were free to think only of his own interests. That's a luxury few of us have when we are dealing with something we can't change. Our lives are usually wrapped up with the lives of others.

As Jesus steeled himself for the cross, he also thought about his disciples. His concern was evident the evening before his trials and his crucifixion.

THE PRAYER THAT MADE A DIFFERENCE

Jesus gathered the disciples in a borrowed room for a final meal together. As they ate the traditional Passover meal, Jesus said there was a traitor in their midst, and then he mentioned a prayer that he had prayed: "Simon, Simon! Listen! Satan has received permission to test all of you, to separate the good from the bad, as a farmer separates the wheat from the chaff. But I have prayed for you, Simon, that your faith will not fail. And when you turn back to me, you must strengthen your brothers" (Luke 22:31–32, TEV).

Talking to Simon Peter, Jesus cautioned them about the hours immediately ahead. They were going to be tested like a farmer separating the grain from the chaff. The future would be turbulent for the disciples and specifically for Peter.

We are not to think that Jesus did not pray for all the disciples, but he singled out Peter. He was in special danger and particularly needed Jesus' help. Jesus' prayer was not that Satan should be prohibited from testing Peter, but rather that his faith wouldn't fail.

Peter responded by proclaiming absolute loyalty to Jesus (Luke 22:23). Peter said he was "ready to go to prison" and "to die" with Jesus. Peter may have expected Jesus to have commended him for his loyalty. Instead, Peter heard a sober prediction. "I tell you, Peter," Jesus said, "the rooster will not crow tonight until you have said three times that you do not know me" (Luke 22:34, TEV).

Peter's loyalty to Jesus would lapse temporarily, but Jesus was confident it would return. He said, "*When* you turn back" not "*if* you turn back." The conjunction is very important in Jesus' statement: "*But* I have prayed for you."

Satan might have been granted power to sift the disciples, but Satan would gain only temporary victory. Peter would deny Jesus, but he would repent and come back a humbler and wiser man because Jesus had prayed.

INTERCESSORY LOVE

Later that same evening, Jesus considered the present and future needs of his disciples. He completed the preparation of those dearest and nearest to him with a final discourse (John 14, 15, 16).

* "I am going to prepare a place for you" (14:2b, TEV).
* "I will ask the Father, and he will give you another Helper" (14:16a, TEV).
* "The Helper, the Holy Spirit . . . will teach you everything, and make you remember all that I have told you" (14:26, TEV).
* "But I chose you from this world, and you do not belong to it; that is why the world hates you" (15:19b, TEV).

Jesus concluded his discourse with a prayer (John 17)— a prayer of loving concern.

Jesus began his prayer by reviewing his mission (John 17:1–5), but his main thrust was for his disciples (John 17:6–19). Jesus expressed gratitude for them (17:6–8), and he expressed concern for what they would be up against in the world. "Holy Father, protect them by the power of your name" (17:11, NIV). Like his prayer for Peter, he didn't ask God to remove them from the struggle, but he did ask that God "protect them from the evil one" (17:15, NIV).

Jesus asked that his disciples be set apart for God's purpose. "Sanctify them by the truth; your word is truth" (17:17, NIV). This would enable them to fulfill the enormous responsibility Jesus was going to give them. Jesus was depending on them to continue his ministry and to tell the story of his sacrificial death.

Confident that God would answer his requests, Jesus saw future believers who would be won through the message and ministry of the disciples (John 17:20). In one comprehensive glance, he saw all those the Father was going to give him. He prayed for them to be united (John 17:21). Unity would be important if believers were to penetrate the world with his message.

Jesus also wanted them "to be with me where I am" (John 17:24b, TEV). Margaret Magdalen, in her book *Jesus, Man of Prayer,* says this "was not merely a prayer for the life beyond this life . . . but for a living relationship with him."[2] Jesus wanted them to have intimate fellowship with him, unhindered by sin.

THE LOVE GOES ON

When Jesus left earth and ascended to the Father, he did not stop praying. What Jesus did for Peter and for the disciples, he does for us. The risen Christ is at the right hand of God, making intercession for us (Rom. 8:34; 1 John 2:1;

Heb. 7:25). Having Jesus as our high priest in heaven is a great comfort.

With so much emphasis put on techniques and faithfulness, prayer can become a burden. Verlene, a woman in a Sunday school class I once taught, desperately wanted a child. Married and childless for eight years, she prayed fervently for one. She told me, "I'm afraid if I miss one day of devotions, God will not give me a baby." She needed to know that the responsibility of praying was not all hers. "We derive now from the soul of Christ the same great support which, during His incarnational life, was the stay of the disciples as they endeavored to love and serve Him."[3]

Jesus sympathizes with and exercises mercy toward us because he knows what human life is like. Jesus experienced every kind of temptation we experience (Heb. 4:15).

> He understands what it means to be subjected to the pressures that induce us to sin. His divine Sonship may have made His personal victory over sin a foregone conclusion but that does not minimize the reality of His temptations, nor the necessity that was laid upon Him to avail Himself of the same means of grace by which we now may triumph. And because He came through temptation victoriously (12:2), . . . so may we by His divine succor (2:18).[4]

Jesus exercises his priestly function without interruption or interference. He is a "priest for ever" (Heb. 7:17), and he "continueth ever," having "an unchangeable priesthood" (Heb. 7:24). Therefore, there is never a single moment when his prayers on our behalf do not reach our heavenly Father. There is never a single moment when he hangs out a "Do Not Disturb" sign. He is always "on call."

The more we know about Jesus' role of intercessor and

the more we acknowledge it, the greater comfort we will experience. Here are some ways we can increase our consciousness of his praying for us.

* We can memorize and recite Bible verses such as Romans 8:34 and Hebrews 7:25 about Jesus' role as intercessor.
* We can meditate on his intercessory role when we take communion. The night Jesus prayed for Peter and for the disciples is when he instituted the Lord's Supper as a memorial meal.
* We can acknowledge his intercessory role when we pray. For example, our prayer may sound like this: "Lord Jesus, I know right now as I am praying that you are praying right along with me. I know you understand my plight because you know what it is like to walk this earth. It is a great comfort to me not to have to carry this burden alone."

Some believers feel uncomfortable addressing their prayers to Jesus or believe it is wrong.[5] We can still recognize Jesus' role by praying, "Heavenly Father, I know that Jesus is there at your right hand. I know you are listening to him as he interprets my case. I trust you to answer and to respond to him as you did to his prayers for Peter and the disciples."

While increasing our awareness of his role comforts us, his intercession is not dependent on our knowledge. His intercession goes on whether or not we're aware of it: "But for the intercession of Jesus there would not necessarily be perpetuity in our faith."[6] "It is his love for us that prevents us from turning him loose altogether in the hour of trial."[7]

TEMPTED TO TURN LOOSE

While Bob aggressively pursued his work as an executive recruiter, I "went to work" trying to figure out what had happened. When I added up three years of seminary, four years of graduate work, four different jobs in higher education, a call to the ministry, and an executive recruiter's job, it made no sense. Because it didn't, I concluded that God had no purpose in it. Overgeneralizing, I concluded that God didn't have a purpose for our lives.

Rolling stones don't gather moss, but ruminating thoughts do. Mentally, I chewed over and over comments people had made such as, "If you just have faith, Bob will get a job. In fact, God probably has a better job waiting for Bob."

To which I mentally responded, *Faith is what got Bob and me into this dilemma. We prayed and sought God's leadership at every step.* If I said as much, then I was accused of having a "negative spirit" and was warned to get my life straightened out.

While some insisted our problem was a lack of faith, others told us that getting a position depended on "who you know." In our attempt to be conscientious Christians, we had not given thought to making "connections" for our future. We were sincere, hard-working Christians. We did our jobs quietly without fanfare, had a simple lifestyle, and were family oriented. Those qualities, we learned, were not good enough to insure success.

Overreacting, I became critical of many of the religious leaders who were deemed successful. It did not seem to matter what kind of life some of these leaders lived. The "sheep" seem to make no distinction over what kind of "shepherd" they followed. If the leader's words were spoken with authority, if they were preceded with, "God told me . . . ," then they were accepted and followed whether or not the words were in accord with the nature and teachings of Jesus. Power and personality in the leader were the important things. It looked as though what it took to succeed in the Christian realm was the same as what it took to succeed in the secular realm—assertiveness, successful image, political connections, being a good promoter and a people-manipulator.

I brooded over how naive I had been to have believed it could have been otherwise. Being conscientious and having a sincere desire to serve the Lord were not enough to keep a job in a Christian setting or to enter the ministry. With the loss of my naivete, I became depressed.

During the week, away from Christians, I would make progress fighting my depression. When I went to church, I would regress when I heard statements like, "God doesn't sponsor losers." Eventually I began to see that my disturbing thoughts were linked with my Christian activities. If I quit going to church, perhaps I could break free from depression's grip.

In my mind's eye, I pictured the Christian activities I would eliminate from my life—Sunday school, morning and evening worship, Bible studies, etc. Then across the picture came Jesus, dusty and bloody, carrying his cross, wearing his crown of thorns, experiencing the ultimate in rejection. With weary, sad eyes, he said to me, "Brenda, I thought we were in this together." With those words and that look, I knew that I could never quit.

I am a Christian today and a faithful church member because Jesus held on to me. His intercessory love was in effect even when I was not aware of it. I'm so glad his life was—and is—still wrapped up in the lives of others.

MAKING YOUR WILL MINE

How does Jesus' intercession for me differ from how others pray for me?

What difference does the fact that Jesus is praying for me make in my ability to cope?

How may I increase my awareness of Jesus' intercessory role?

"Thou art a priest for ever. . . ."[8]
"Ever for us interceding. . . ."[9]

CHAPTER 13

EXPRESSING EMOTIONS: A NECESSARY RELEASE

I had been lamenting the wounds of my childhood and parading them before God. As self-pity overthrew me, I wept violent tears held back for 20 years. I accused God of injustice.
"He crushed me," I shouted aloud, "and you stood by watching! He rejected me, and you remained silent . . ."
For an hour or more the bitterness flowed, till my eyes were swollen. When I finally collapsed into silence, the Lord answered me.[1]

PAUL THIGPEN

Sometimes when a boxer, famous for his strength and past victories, climbs into the ring, his fans chant, "Easy, easy!" They expect him to knock his opponent out in a few rounds.

"We need to be aware of building up an image of Jesus in which he is a 'star' for whom the fight is easy."[2] Jesus was perfectly obedient, but not without effort. He was "not programmed like an automaton so that he *could not* disobey. Every act of obedience was a response of the will, not a conditioned reflex."[3]

As we've walked with Jesus during this study, we've witnessed some of the "rounds" he fought, but none was as intense as the one in the Garden of Gethsemane. After confidently and lovingly meeting the needs of the disciples, he moved to the garden to deal with his own needs. He took the apostles with him.

BEING IN AGONY

Jesus had the apostles wait while he and Peter, James, and John proceeded deeper into the garden. At this point, Matthew says, Jesus "*began* to be sorrowful and very heavy (Matt. 26:37b, emphasis added)." Mark says that Jesus "*began* to be sore amazed, and to be very heavy" (Mark 14:33b, emphasis added). The word *began* indicates the commencement of a new level of sorrow more severe in degree than Jesus had ever experienced before![4]

"Sorrowful" (Matt. 26:37) and "sore amazed" (Mark 14:33) carry the idea of sorrow to the point of great amazement. The word *terrified* would be a good translation.[5]

Jesus said to Peter, James, and John, "The sorrow in my heart is so great that it almost crushes me" (Mark 14:34, TEV). Jesus had reached a stage of anguish that was approaching the utmost limit of endurance.[6]

Jesus went on further, beyond Peter, James, and John, and prayed. Luke describes Jesus as kneeling in prayer (22:41). Matthew describes him as prostrate upon the ground (26:39), and Mark used a verb tense that indicates repeated or continuous action (Mark 14:35).[7] If we put all three of these together, Jesus probably first fell to his knees, and as the struggle intensified, he repeatedly threw himself to the ground.

In great emotional distress, Jesus prayed, "My Father, if it is possible, take this cup of suffering from me!" (Matt. 26:39b, TEV).

This short prayer probably represents the essence of what Jesus actually was praying, because those with Jesus fell asleep while he prayed. Jesus said to Peter, "How is it that you three were not able to keep watch with me for even one hour?" (Matthew 26:40, TEV). He then wearily returned to his place of prayer and repeated his request. His praying did not bring immediate relief. In fact, the struggle intensified, and an angel appeared to strengthen Jesus (Luke 22:43).

Still, the misery continued. "And being in an agony he prayed more earnestly" (Luke 22:44). " 'Being in an agony' . . . conveys the idea of growing intensity. Christ had progressed in struggle from the first prayer into an even more intensive combat."[8]

The combat was so intense that "his sweat was as . . . great drops of blood falling down to the ground" (Luke 22:44). Under great stress, tiny capillaries in the sweat glands can break, mixing the blood and the sweat. This process alone is enough to produce marked weakness and possible shock.

THE CUP OF SUFFERING

In his anguish, Jesus cried out to God for some alternative. Three times Jesus prayed that the "cup of suffering" be taken from him. Bible commentators disagree over what the "cup" was.

* Jesus was a healthy young man who resisted death as any mentally healthy person would. The desire to live is built into our human nature. No one wishes to die; no one wishes to die at thirty-three. While Jesus had known all along that he must die, he had a natural resistance to it as the time grew short.
* The "cup" could have been the rejection and public execution Jesus would have to experience. To die on the cross, he must surrender himself to dreadful shame, to abuse, and to excruciating pain.
* Others say Jesus was not disturbed by the prospect of physical torture. Rather, he dreaded the heinousness of becoming the scapegoat, the sacrificial lamb who would bear the sins of the world.

Whatever the "cup" was, Jesus faced it with dread. He was seeking *a way out* from the Father. In one sense, escape routes *were* open to Jesus. If they weren't, that would have made a mockery of his willingly choosing to die for us (John 10:17–18). In the darkness of the night, he could have slipped out of Jerusalem. He could have compromised with the religious leaders and diluted their hostility. He could have called on regiments of angels to come to his defense (Matt. 26:51–54).

In another sense though, escape wasn't possible. This is what makes his struggle so complex. Jesus wanted to do what God wanted. "Yet not what I want, but what you want" (Matt. 26:39c, TEV). Jesus knew the cross was essential to the plan, purpose, and design of God, whom he wanted to please. If he wanted to be the obedient Son, escape was not possible.

Jesus dealt with both sides of the tension that existed and wrestled within him by praying. He prayed for an escape, and he acknowledged his desire to please God.

GOD'S RESPONSE

God responded by giving Jesus a way *through* rather than a way *out*. After Jesus' plea for escape, God strengthened him in such a way that Jesus calmly proceeded toward the cross. As the drama of his last hours unfolded, Jesus, more than Pilate, more than those who sought his arrest, appeared to be in control. Throughout the entire course of the arrest and trial, Jesus was the picture of a man on top of the situation. The emotional states of Jesus when he entered the garden that night and when he later left in chains to be tried and crucified were entirely different. Something happened in the garden that radically changed Jesus' emotional condition. He "left the garden with quiet confidence to accomplish the Father's will."[9]

IMPORTANT LESSONS FROM GETHSEMANE

1. From Jesus' experience we learn that the struggle with what we can't change can become very intense. This is not a given, but some of us may find ourselves in agony. We experience a depth of feeling that we didn't know existed. We may experience sorrow in our hearts so great that it almost crushes us (Matt. 26:38b).

2. We learn that some battles repeat themselves. On Monday, Jesus had admitted he was stirred and agitated. He prayed, "Father, glorify thy name" (John 12:28a). He was

helped by the prayer; but by Thursday night, the struggle was back.

This doesn't mean we can't—or won't—win the war. It just means we shouldn't be surprised when a battle reoccurs. Neither does it mean that we should discount the gain or relief experienced at any one battle. God gives us what we need at each critical juncture. That the battle comes back simply indicates the nature of what we are up against.

3. Jesus' experience in Gethsemane shows how much emotion is wrapped up with the spiritual. Surrendering to God's will was—and is—basically a spiritual struggle, but emotions are involved. Jesus' experience shows that the feelings that accompany unchangeables may be intense; they may be agonizing, but they are normal.

Jesus didn't see his emotions as something to hide. If he did, he would not have taken his disciples with him to the garden. His emotional struggle took nothing away from him as a person. If anything, it enhanced him. It makes me appreciate all the more what it cost him to die on the cross. The fight was never "easy."

4. The two-fold nature of Jesus' prayer shows us that he admitted his struggle to God. He felt no need for cover-up or pretense. If Jesus, who knew the Father intimately, offered his prayer in this manner, then we should feel free to do likewise.

There is no need to hide our emotions from God, since he is aware of their existence even before we are (Matt. 6:8). The Bible says that "all things are naked and opened unto the eyes of him with whom we have to do" (Heb. 4:13b), so we do not need to conceal anything from God. With reverence and respect, we may bare our hearts before him and tell him how we feel.

Ronald Dunn discovered this valuable and liberating truth in the aftermath of the death of his son. He writes, "I learned. . . . It's okay to tell God how you feel. After all, He already knows. I've never told God anything He didn't already know. I've never heard God gasp in surprise at anything I said. I've never heard God say in response to any confession, 'I would never have believed that of you.' "[10]

5. Jesus offered up his prayers with "strong crying and tears" (Heb. 5:7). He released his emotions, something we may be reluctant to do. The emotions that accompany what we can't change may be unpleasant ones, like anger, grief, or fear. Because they feel so terrible, we might be tempted to keep the lid on them rather than let them surface, but they need to be released. Ignoring them can set us up for further difficulties, and their presence can prevent God's help from getting through.

John M. Koessler was the product of a dysfunctional family, something he couldn't change. In a *Decision* magazine article, Koessler described how he hid his emotions rather than releasing them. He stuffed them into a "secret closet hidden in the dark recesses" of his soul.[11] "Eventually the closet became too full to accept another repressed emotion, and my repressed emotions started tumbling out. If I allowed myself the liberty of a little anger, it swelled into a torrent of rage. A moment of sadness spiraled into deep depression."[12]

Failure to release the emotions that accompany what we can't change may set us up for depression, cynicism, deep bitterness, chronic irritability, and even medical problems. Even worse, unreleased emotions can block our channel for receiving supernatural help.

Unreleased emotions swell, filling the channel God needs to minister to us. Releasing our emotions opens up the channel so God can respond. As Karen Burton Mains writes, "How many times he refused to respond to my prayer requests, often for weeks or months. Then when I finally spilled forth my anguished frustrations, suddenly the heavens opened and he overwhelmed me with his love."[13]

A crusty magazine reporter discovered this when he was dying from a hepatitis virus that was destroying his liver. As a journalism student, he had been taught to be objective. He had learned not to express emotions. A lay hospital chaplain told him, "Don't be afraid to show your feelings. God gave us tears to wash our pain away."

After the reporter learned to express his emotions in prayer, he said that in a way nothing had changed. He was still going to die. But in another sense, everything changed because he now had hope. He believed he could grow and gain from the experience ahead.[14]

6. Jesus prayed for an escape. It seems odd to suggest praying for escape from something we can't change, yet it helps. Knowing something is unchangeable causes us to fight against it rather than accept it. This continual resistance creates a pressure buildup and increases the difficulty of adjustment. Praying for an escape releases the pressure. It's an emotional release valve. Once the pressure is released, the repressed emotions can escape, clearing the channel for God to respond.

When I discussed this concept with a friend, she said, "My prayer journal is filled with escape requests. Some of those pleas were granted, but the majority were not. God, however, always gave me the grace and strength to deal with what I couldn't change." When the pressure was released, when the emotions were honestly expressed, God strengthened her just as he did Jesus and just as he wants to strengthen us.

MAKING YOUR WILL MINE

What is so awful about what I can't change that makes me
want to escape?

What emotions am I experiencing?

Why am I hesitant to express those feelings in prayer?

Why would expressing my feelings in prayer help me?

*"Father . . . my Father! All things are possible for you.
Take this cup of suffering from me! Yet not what I want,
but what you want."*[15]

CHAPTER 14

"FATHER, FORGIVE THEM . . ."

When you forgive, you reclaim your power to
choose. It doesn't matter whether someone deserves
forgiveness; you deserve to be free.[1]

MARY GRUNTE

Jesus had just finished his prayer battle in the Garden of Gethsemane when a large crowd arrived. They were armed with swords and clubs and were intent on finding him. Judas, one of Jesus' apostles, was their leader. He had arranged a signal with them, "The man I kiss is the one you want" (see Matt. 26:48).

When Judas kissed him, Jesus said, "Is it with a kiss that you betray the Son of Man?" (see Luke 22:48).

The chief priests, the elders, and the temple police arrested Jesus, and all the disciples left him and ran away (Matt. 26:55–56).

The crowd whisked Jesus away for some hastily arranged trials before the Sanhedrin, the governing body of the Jews. Ignoring their own judicial standards, the religious leaders didn't seek any witnesses on Jesus' behalf. They paid false witnesses to testify against him and found him guilty on false charges. Then they took him to the Roman procurator, Pontius Pilate—a step necessary to legally bring about Jesus' death.

Pilate sensed that Jesus was innocent, but not wanting to court disfavor with the Jews, he tried to avoid making a decision. He sent Jesus to Herod Antipas, tetrarch from Galilee, who was in Jerusalem for the Passover. Herod sent Jesus back to Pilate. Roman soldiers tormented Jesus during his appearances before both Pilate and Herod. They stripped him of his clothes and forced him to wear a crown of thorns.

Still convinced of Jesus' innocence but wanting to please the Jews, Pilate gave the crowd a choice. "Which one do you want me to set free for you? Jesus Barabbas or Jesus called the Christ?" (Matt. 27:17b, TEV).

" 'Barabbas!' they answered" (Matt. 27:21b, TEV).

" 'What, then, shall I do with Jesus called the Messiah?' Pilate asked them" (Matt. 27:22a, TEV).

" 'Crucify him!' they all answered" (Matt. 27:22b, TEV).

Pilate gave in and sentenced Jesus to death (Luke 23:24). Pilate had Jesus whipped and then turned him over to his executioners. They immediately took him to the crucifixion site.

Jesus' hands were nailed (and probably tied) securely to the horizontal bar of the cross. He was hoisted between two thieves. His feet were twisted and a long spike driven through them to the cross. In this position, he could barely move.

But he was a miracle worker, wasn't he? Couldn't he do a superman stunt, flex his muscles and come down from the cross? That's what the passersby wanted to know. They "shouted abuse, shaking their heads in mockery. 'Ha! Look at you now!' they yelled at him. 'You can destroy the Temple and rebuild it in three days, can you? Well then, save yourself, and come down from the cross!' " (Mark 15:29b–30, NLT).

But Jesus didn't save himself. His hour had come. He was caught tightly in the vise of what he could not change. In its clutches, how did Jesus respond to betrayal, desertion, unfairness, ridicule, and pain?

He prayed, "Father, forgive them; for they know not what they do" (Luke 23:34).

It's the same response that some of us need to make.

WHO NEEDS TO FORGIVE?

Not everyone who struggles with unchangeables will need to forgive, but some will.

* Cynthia barely looked up when her husband yelled good-bye on his way out of the door. George was running late for a business appointment in the next town, but Cynthia wasn't concerned. It was a clear day, and the roads were dry so George should make good time. Fifty-five minutes later, a policeman was at her door. "I'm sorry, ma'am, but your husband has been in a terrible accident on the interstate. He was killed."

Cynthia braced herself against the door frame to keep from falling. "What happened?" she asked.

"We don't know why, but a truck was traveling the wrong way on the interstate. As best as we can determine, your husband didn't see him coming because he was behind several cars. When he pulled out to pass, there was the truck, and the two collided. Your husband died instantly. The truck driver is still alive at this time, but his injuries are very serious."

* Karl and Thomas and their wives were the kind of friends who often spent evenings talking after a good meal while their children played nearby. Thomas admitted in one of those talk sessions that he was worried about losing his job. He said, "No matter how hard I try, I can't seem to please my boss."

Considering his friend's skills, Karl said, "Don't worry. If it should come to that, I'll find you a place where I work." Thomas relaxed. He knew he could count on his friend.

Six months later when Thomas was fired, Karl said, "What a tough break. I'll be praying for you." Not a word was said about a job.

* Trudy was a pretty little girl, sweet and cuddly. Everyone wanted to hold her and to play with her when her large, extended family gathered for reunions. Uncle Lawrence, though, was the only one who took her for long walks. He took her to the pasture to see the cows and behind the barn to look at the little piggies. Out of sight from other family members, he fondled her in inappropriate ways. Trudy's innocence was robbed by a man who knew better.

Incidents such as the three above leave us struggling with various emotions.

> * *Anger.* Cynthia was angry. How could a person be so careless to drive the wrong way on an interstate, risking the lives of many and killing George? Now her children were fatherless, and she was left without a husband.

Trudy, too, was angry. Her anger had been simmering for years. How could her uncle have abused her? Why didn't her parents protect her? Why didn't some other relative notice what was happening and rescue her?

* *Demand for justice.* Our hearts cry out for justice when we have been wronged. Uncle Lawrence ought to be punished. The reckless truck driver should have to pay with his life.

* *Grief.* Cynthia's loss was great. She wept for herself, for her children, and for the life they would have had if George had lived.

Thomas grieved over Karl's silence. He thought more about Karl's promise than he did about what he couldn't change—the job he had lost, or what he could change—getting a new job. How could his friend forget so quickly what he had said? How could he ignore his situation?

Initially, these emotions are healthy responses if we release them in appropriate ways. (Honest praying, we've learned, is a healthy release.) But if we don't release these emotions, then we may "grow" another problem: unforgiveness.

Our grief turns into bitterness or cynicism. Our anger intensifies and smolders. Our legitimate desire for justice turns into a desire for revenge. We nurse our hurt by reliving the wrong over and over, robbing us of peace of mind. Unforgiveness distorts our vision, warps our thinking, and pollutes our soul. The pain and the hurt control us.

The obvious remedy for escaping this bondage is forgiveness.

* It breaks the ruminating cycle.
* It frees up energy.
* It restores peace of mind.
* It renews our vision.
* It removes the venom poisoning our souls.
* It enables us to move forward instead of holding on to the past.

With so many benefits, why do we hesitate to forgive?

We may hesitate because the bondage itself is so strong. Already caught in the vise of what we can't change, unforgiveness tightens its grip. To break that kind of bondage is tough to do.

We may hesitate because forgiveness ignores our own hurt. It suggests that anything can happen to us or be done to us, and it is not important.

Another reason we hesitate to forgive is that we fear the forgiven will not have to be accountable or punished. We equate forgiveness with saying, "Oh, never mind. It's all right. What you did doesn't really matter."

I sympathize with these hesitancies so much that I was reluctant to write this chapter. And yet if we are going to walk with Jesus all the way from his baptism to the cross, this is a step we must imitate. Unless we forgive, our coping with what we can't change won't be complete. We won't experience peace of mind or be able to move forward in life. We'll put a limit on the amount of help God can give us.

IMITATING JESUS

Jesus' prayer of forgiveness does not tell us everything we need to know about forgiving, but it does give us some important help.

1. *Start where you are and not where you should be.* Jesus didn't pray, "Father, help me to forgive those who have brought about my death and mistreated me." Instead, he prayed, "Father, forgive them . . ."

These are good words for us to use in getting started. We do not have to feel like forgiving to initiate the process. We do not have to begin with "*I* forgive"; we can begin with "*Father,* forgive them." When we take the right actions, the right emotions will follow.

This is not to suggest that Jesus wasn't expressing his forgiveness when he prayed. Earlier in his ministry, he had taught, "Pray for those who abuse you" (see Luke 6:28), and on the cross, he did exactly that.

His example, though, suggests a tool for us to use. When we don't have the words to say, when we don't have the heart to forgive, praying Jesus' words will get us started.

2. *Acknowledge God's sovereign rule.* Jesus prayed for God's forgiveness for his tormentors and executioners because they were going to need it. Jesus knew that those who abused him and ridiculed him would be held accountable for their actions. This is verified by early New Testament preachers. They tried to stab men's minds with the realization of the sheer crime of the cross. Every mention of the crucifixion in Acts is instinctive with horror at the crime committed (cf. Acts 2:23; 3:13; 4:10; 5:30).

Praying "Father, forgive them" acknowledges that what people do does matter. In a world where men and women hurl injustices on others, God will hold them accountable and execute punishment (Rom. 12:19).

We have laws and legal options that help us make each other accountable, but those have their limits. Cynthia discovered this when she brought a civil suit against the truck driver who killed her husband. She won a large settlement because of his negligence, but it wasn't enough to eliminate her bitterness. She knew she had to release the driver to God, the one whom we are all ultimately accountable to. She didn't feel like forgiving the truck driver, but she asked God to. She prayed "Father, forgive him" because it was the right thing to do. It is what Jesus would have done. As she disciplined herself to pray those words day after day, eventually her bitterness melted and she embraced life.

3. *Try to gain insight concerning those who wronged you.* In his prayer asking God to forgive those who wronged him, Jesus included a significant phrase: "For they know not what they do" (Luke 23:34). Jesus looked upon those who wanted him to die as victims of a system. They were blinded by the ceremonial restrictions of the law. They were blinded by years of tradition of what they perceived God to be like, blinded by what was really a fabrication. Jesus looked and saw them responding to the circumstances and forces around them. They were unaware of the dreadful consequences of their act. They did not, in their ignorance, know that they were bringing suffering and death to the Son of God.

If we can gain insight concerning those who have wronged us, we gain a valuable tool for forgiving them. What forces shaped their lives? What drove them to do what they did? If we could know all that is in their hearts, if we could walk in their shoes for a while, perhaps seeing some of the their pain, we might be more tender in our judgment.

I wonder if this isn't one reason why Jesus suggested confrontation when forgiveness is needed (Matt. 18:15; Luke 17:3). Confrontation leads to communication. In talking with the person who wronged us, we may gain understanding of the forces that shaped and motivated him or her.

In order to forgive Karl, Thomas decided he would have to confront him—let him know how he had hurt him. He asked Karl to meet him for coffee. Thomas said, "I don't understand how you forgot about your offer to get me a job. Did I misunderstand?"

Karl answered, "No, you didn't misunderstand. As it turned out, I don't have as much influence at work as I thought I did. In fact, I'm now worried about my own job. Things are shaky and unsettled at the office. Everyone is suspicious of each other. I shouldn't have said what I did to you that night. Afterwards, I was ashamed to admit to you how little influence I have."

Hearing those words, Thomas saw that his friend hadn't deliberately meant to hurt him, and he forgave him. Thomas was able to take the emotional energy he had been using for ruminating and channel it into his search for a new job.

Trudy, though, couldn't confront Uncle Lawrence because he died when she was a teenager. The counselor she was seeing for depression suggested that she find out what she could about Uncle Lawrence's past. After some discreet investigation, Trudy discovered that he had been the victim of sexual abuse and that he had trouble relating to adults. Making this discovery wasn't the only tool Trudy used to forgive him, but it was an important one. It broke that incessant ruminating which contributed to the smoldering fire of unforgiveness. Over and over she had asked, How could he do such a thing? Now she knew.

Forgiveness does not suggest that wrongdoers go unpunished, but it does call for understanding of the pressures that lead to the transgression. When the unforgiving spirit is threatening to turn our hearts to bitterness, let us hear again Jesus praying for forgiveness for those who crucified him, and let us follow his example. When we do, we'll be able to let go of our painful emotions and move on with our lives.

MAKING YOUR WILL MINE

Recognizing when unforgiveness is a problem:

Have I found myself saying, "You don't know how unbearable my suffering has been! You don't know how much I've been hurt!"?

Am I jealous of others whose lives appear to be easier, smoother, or more successful?

Am I quick to claim my rights?

Am I sensitive to wrongs done to me, however slight, as if I had exposed nerves over my entire body?

Have I exploded with rage when I thought I had everything under control?

Have friends or family members looked embarrassed or changed the subject when I talk about what happened?

When trying to come to terms with what I can't change, why do I need to consider forgiveness?

How can Jesus' example help me to forgive when it seems impossible?

What can I pray when I can't say, "I forgive"?

"Lord, do not hold this sin against them."[2]

CHAPTER 15

TOTALLY ABANDONED?

[Jesus] did not for one minute fail in obedience, yet he dared to ask "Why?" He did not curse God like his neighbor on the cross. But he questioned him. And that is consolation indeed to those of us who have cried out "Why?"[1]

MARGARET MAGDALEN

Have you ever noticed how problems appear more manageable in daylight than in the darkness? How pain is more bearable in the daytime than in the night? There's something about darkness that exaggerates problems and pain and makes them worse.

At noon, after Jesus had hung on the cross since nine o'clock, a thick darkness settled over the earth. In the awful darkness, Jesus shouted, "Eloi, Eloi, lama sabachthani?" (Mark 15:34).

We thought Jesus had already endured all a person could endure, and now comes the awful cry, "My God, my God, why hast thou forsaken me?"

"It was not a whisper or a monotone but a loud cry."[2] We want to cover our ears to keep from hearing it. If Jesus could be forsaken by God, does that mean we could be too?

JESUS' MYSTERIOUS PRAYER

If we take the prayer at its face value, the prayer represents a response of despair to severe testing. Many Bible interpreters cannot fathom Jesus making this kind of response. The words of this prayer are taken directly from Psalm 22:1, so some say Jesus was quoting it in confidence and trust as death neared. Psalm 22 begins in despair and ends on a triumphant note, but many psalms have the same pattern. I am more inclined to agree with William Barclay, who says, "On a cross a man does not repeat poetry to himself, even the poetry of a psalm."[3]

Other Bible scholars say Jesus felt forsaken because he was bearing the sins of the world. Sin separates us from God. Up to this moment Jesus had gone through every experience of life except being separated from God because of sin. Jesus had never experienced this because he was without sin. Feeling the weight of the burden that was his as he took on the sins of the whole world, Jesus knew what it meant to be a sinner. His fellowship with God, which had already sustained him, was briefly clouded. Jesus' prayer expressed the wretched feeling of broken fellowship.

Elton Trueblood writes that the loneliness must have been almost unbearable for Jesus. It is true that we often count on the support of fellow believers to help us through difficult times. We credit their support as God's doing; his way of letting us know he is with us. When we don't have that kind of support, loneliness engulfs us. Jesus had little support at the cross. Trueblood states, "The crowd, instead of being moved to compassion by His suffering, were either idly curious or openly glad that He was in torment. Instead of compassion which He needed at this point, He received ridicule."[4]

Jesus was scoffed by the crowd and the soldiers. Some women followers stood at a distance, but "where were the Twelve to whom He had given His closest attention? Where were the members of the innermost circle, once gathered for prayer on the Mountain of Transfiguration?"[5] The darkness accentuated his loneliness.

In my research, I did not find one Bible interpreter who connected Jesus' cry of abandonment to the physical torture of the crucifixion. While he might have experienced terrible loneliness and while he might have known for the first time the consequence of sin, he never agonized over the confining and excruciating pain of the cross.

In overlooking the pain of the cross, I think Bible interpreters may be missing another possible explanation. Long iron nails were driven between the bones of his wrists into the wood crossbar. The nails usually tore through the median nerve. This would have created an unending trail of fire up his arms, augmenting the pain from the long spike through his ankles. The rigidity of his position caused muscle cramps. Dehydration created unbearable thirst.

Jesus was already so weak from the whipping he received preceding the crucifixion that the Roman soldiers had to tap Simon of Cyrene to carry his cross (Luke 23:26; Mark 15:21). Now, nailed to the cross, he couldn't even swipe at the gnats and flies that swarmed around the dried blood on his head and back. He couldn't wipe the sweat from his forehead. He was experiencing a degree of agony exceeding that of Gethsemane.

Excruciating pain for hours at a time can make a person

feel abandoned by God, as many cancer patients will tell you. To me, it takes nothing away from Jesus' humanity or his divinity if he cried out because of the physical torture of the crucifixion. If his pain reached the point of making him feel abandoned by God, that makes his sacrifice (and love) for me all the greater.

Perhaps the explanation for Jesus' mysterious prayer isn't *one* of these, but *all* of them. The spiritual, emotional, and physical ramifications of the cross pressed in on him. In the darkness they were magnified in such a way as to make him feel abandoned. He expressed his forsakenness with a scriptural prayer.

Many of life's experiences, especially those in which we feel forsaken by God, are not neat and tidy. Many variables enter the picture. They overlap and interlace in such a way that we end up feeling isolated and confused.

MULTIPLE REASONS, MULTIPLE HURTS

When I am asked why I became depressed, I answer, "A loss of purpose." While that was the bottom line of my depression, other variables were involved:

* The many rejections we received when Bob tried to enter the ministry, even from our own church. Too much of my self-esteem was wrapped up in what other Christians thought of me.
* Faulty thinking patterns. People with ruminating response styles are more prone to depression. I'm a first-class ruminator.
* Unexpressed emotion. It provides fertile ground for growing depression. I held my despair in.

* Physical strength. The hardest time for me was late
  in the afternoons, when I experienced what I refer
  to as the "four o'clock blues." That was also when
  I was very tired from the day's work and was trying to fix dinner for the family.

Eventually I sought professional help for my depression
and made good progress, except for those pesky "four
o'clock blues." Confusion would roll in and the bleak sadness of depression would cover me.

One afternoon, I was peeling potatoes when the sadness descended. I thought, *I've got to do something about
this.* I put down my paring knife and went to the bathroom.
With the door locked, I knelt by the tub and cried, "God,
how could you do this to us? How could you hurt us when
we've tried so hard to serve you?" Without realizing it, Jesus'
cry from the cross had been imprinted on my mind through
my writing project (see chap. 10). I prayed his prayer just as
he had prayed the psalmist's prayer. After a few afternoons
of praying this way, the "four o'clock blues" ceased, and I
no longer felt abandoned by God.

The emotional intensity of that first afternoon surprised
me. As the tears flowed, I cried over and over again, "How
could you do this to us?" I had held and packed in the hurt
for so long that when I let it go, it gushed forth.

This kind of emotional intensity is not necessary to expressing our abandonment. What is important is that we
express it. How we do it will vary according to the individual and according to the circumstances. For pastor J. Grant
Swank Jr., it was a simple arm gesture.

Swank had resigned his pastorate so he could move his
ailing wife thousands of miles for treatment by a particular

neurosurgeon.[6] After the surgery, recovery did not go well. Priscilla suffered a nervous collapse.

Swank took a job as a staff person for the chamber of commerce. At the end of every workday he would come into the house to find his wife no better. " 'Darkness' fell long before nightfall most evenings."[7]

As days moved into weeks, and weeks into months, Swank wondered, "Will I ever return to the pastorate? Will Priscilla ever recover fully? Will our marriage ever be completely restored? Will life ever return to what it once was?"[8]

Both he and his wife felt separated from friends and from God. "Well-meaning friends would stop by the house to visit. . . . They would laugh, joke and have fun, but that didn't mesh with our present circumstances. The buoyancy in their lives seemed to expose the desperation in our own."[9]

One night as Swank lay in bed unable to sleep, he *reached his arms up into the air.* "I couldn't see my arms because of the darkness. Yet I wanted to reach out and touch God somehow. I did not understand why I felt so alone, so unable to make contact with heaven."[10]

"I persisted in reaching out in the night, touching nothing, feeling nothing. I had not cried in months, and now I could not shed a tear. I was beyond crying. I was not even able to weep before the Lord. 'Where have You gone?' I asked softly, not wanting to appear disrespectful."[11]

At first, his life seemed just as flat as ever after his reach-out-to-touch God prayers. "But I realized," he said, "that I did still trust God."[12]

Gradually Priscilla's health returned, and Swank was able to become a pastor once again. One Sunday night as he lay in bed thinking back over their season of trial, it came to him, "When I had put that childlike question to my

Father: 'Where have You gone?' his answer had come just as simply: 'I have been with you all the time.' "[13]

How can that be when Swank felt so abandoned? Facts and feelings aren't always the same. The Bible promises us that God will never leave us or forsake us (Deut. 31:6; Josh. 1:5; Heb. 13:5). That's true even though we sometimes feel forsaken.

GOD WAS THERE

While Jesus *felt* forsaken, events around the cross reveal that God did not abandon him.

* *The supernatural darkness.* What nature did at this time shows us God's heart. Jesus' death was so terrible that the sky was unnaturally darkened, as if nature could not bear to look.

* *Death came in a short time.* Because no major organs were affected, crucifixion was usually a slow death. It sometimes took days. Jesus died in six hours. It was as if God were saying, "The cross may be necessary, but I'll not have you suffer any longer than is necessary."

* *Shout of triumph.* After his cry of abandonment, Jesus gave a victorious shout (Matt. 27:50; Mark 15:37; Luke 23:46): "It is finished" (John 19:30). In the Greek, that would have been one word: "Finished!" It was the shout of a man who had completed the task, a man who had won through the struggle, a man who had come out of darkness into light. Jesus died with the cry of triumph on his lips, his task accomplished, his work completed, his victory won.

* *The splitting of the veil in the temple.* God responded as a Jewish father would at the death of his son.[14] When Jacob saw the multicolored coat of his beloved Joseph drenched in blood, he rent his garment as an expression of

deepest sorrow. When Job got the shocking news of the death of his children, he tore his clothes as a symbol of his anguish.

"When Jesus bowed His head and died, God rent the veil from top to bottom, symbolically exposing His heart of sorrow—His suffering love."[15]

"By that vivid gesture, God indicated to Jesus' followers that He had personally been close by during the whole, terrible ordeal. God is not distant and unfeeling. He did not coldly send His Son to a cross."[16]

Taken together, these events tell us that "God did not turn his back on Jesus, as some theology has it. God was never nearer than at Golgotha, as Jesus gave himself in full obedience to the Father's will."[17]

When we do not understand, when we cannot see how God could possibly be at work in our circumstances, then we can pray as Jesus prayed, "My God, my God, why have you forsaken me?" What you will discover is what Pastor Swank and I both discovered: God was there all the time.

MAKING YOUR WILL MINE

How is Jesus' cry of abandonment from the cross both awful and consoling?

What are some ways I can express my feelings of abandonment?

What will I discover when I honestly express what I am feeling and thinking?

"Save me, O God!
The water is up to my neck;
I am sinking in deep mud,
and there is no solid ground;
I am out in deep water,
and the waves are about to drown me.
I am worn out from calling for help."[18]

PART III

THE RESOLUTION

Release and Peace

*"Unless a grain of wheat falls into the ground
and dies,
it remains a single grain. But if it does die,
it yields a great harvest."*

JOHN 12:24B, WILLIAMS TRANSLATION

CHAPTER 16

"INTO THY HANDS . . ."

*Here's something you can't dream your way out
of, I told myself. Here's something you can't think
your way out of, buy your way out of, or work
your way out of.
It was all too clear. . . . This is, I thought to myself,
something you can only trust your way out of.*[1]

BOB BUFORD, IN RESPONSE TO HIS

SON'S DEATH

At God's direction, Mark (from chaps. 1 and 2) enrolled
in a community college after being fired from his book-
selling job. Uncertain at first what his new career would be,
he began with computer courses—programming and main-
tenance as well as application courses. He had used computers for years, but now he enjoyed learning the behind-
the-activity part of computers. Soon he was hooked. He got
a part-time job with a computer business while he finished
his degree in computer technology. The week after he grad-
uated, his boss hired him to manage the business. Mark
couldn't have been happier. He was so glad he didn't have

151

to travel any more. One evening over coffee, he said to his wife, "Being fired was one of the best things that ever happened to me."

Six years after the Christian university told Bob they would not renew his contract, we received a call from Bill, a pastor-friend in another state. The previous Sunday Bill had been absent from his pulpit and had asked a Christian college president to fill in for him. When Bill got back to his office, he played the tape of the president's message. The president had said they were looking for people to fill two administrative positions they had open.

Knowing our situation, Bill called immediately. He was so excited. He said, "I think this is it."

And it was. Bob wrote the college for a job description, applied, and in a few months had one of the jobs. What happened to us was like a peculiar parenthesis. As suddenly as the bizarre job difficulties started, they ended, and my husband has been happily employed as a college administrator ever since.

The way Mark's and Bob's stories end is how we would like all of our stories to end. We would like our struggle with what we can't change to make sense. We would like to think that our own parenthesis in life will close, and things will be the way they once were. Unfortunately, our stories may end differently.

* *Even when we pray Jesus' way, our situation may still not make sense.* We can withdraw to lonely places, we can express gratitude and we can be honest about our emotions, and still not have that sense of rightness that Mark experienced. This doesn't take anything away from the relief the tools bring. They enabled us to cope even when the "why" escaped us.

* *Some situations defy an explanation—at least, in this*

life. Edmund was twenty-six years old when he was diagnosed with amyotrophic lateral sclerosis (ALS, or Lou Gehrig's disease). His neurologist told him, "You have six to twelve months to live." Death was inevitable. Sitting in his wheelchair day after day, Edmund wondered, "Why me? I'm too young to have my life end. This doesn't make any sense."

In cases like Edmund's, we think of all we wanted in life. We become preoccupied with "what might have been" or "what never will be." We stew over what appears to be God's unfairness.

* *Even when we pray Jesus' way, our situation may not be reversible, where we can go back to the way things were.* The limb that was amputated cannot be sewed back on, the eye that was lost cannot be replaced, and the child who died will not be coming back. While we may be coping outwardly, inwardly we may become resentful. We make a partial adjustment using Jesus' tools, but not a complete adjustment. A spiritual residue lingers, robbing us of inner peace.

For those who do not have an explanation for their situation and for those whose situation is not reversible, there remains a final challenge. Can we give to God what we can't change?

"INTO THY HANDS . . ."

After his prayer of abandonment, fellowship was restored between Jesus and the Father. Jesus said, "It is finished!" (John 19:30b, NASB). All that Jesus had done, sought, hoped for, loved, and dreamed were finished. He had accomplished what the Father called him to do. His work was finished. All that he could do had been done; all that he could give had been given. "And when Jesus had cried with a loud voice, he said, Father, into thy hands I commend my spirit: and having said thus, he gave up the ghost" (Luke 23:46).

From his first prayer, he knew his mission and his destiny, and he could die knowing he had achieved what God wanted him to achieve. "Here, Father, I give you my life. I give you my work."[2]

When we've done all we can do about our situation, when we have wrestled with it and lost sleep over it, we can give it to God. It's the attitude—the trust inherent in Jesus' prayer—that we want to emulate.

THE PRAYER OF TRUST

Commend means to entrust, to deliver with confidence, to give as a deposit for trust or safekeeping. Jesus' obedience all through his life had been a lovely thing, and now, even though he has experienced the cross and abandonment, he deposits his life into the hands of God.

The words of Jesus' prayer come from Psalm 31:5: "Into thine hand I commit my spirit." Jews often used this phrase as a prayer by adding the word, "Father." It was the first prayer every Jewish mother taught her child to say when he lay down to sleep at night, before the threatening dark came. Perhaps Mary had taught the prayer to Jesus. When he was dying, Jesus prayed the prayer he had prayed many times as a little boy.[3]

Following the prayer, Jesus bowed his head and died. "John says that Jesus leaned back His head and gave up His spirit. The word that John uses is the word which might be used for settling back upon a pillow. For Jesus the strife was over and the battle was won."[4] So there came to Jesus the peace after his long battle, rest after his earnest work, and contentment knowing he had completed his task. With the sure and restful sigh of a tired child, he died confident of his Father's care.

This peace is what we want. We want to be confident of the Father's care and to be able to rest in him. We want our inner agitation about what we can't change to cease, and it will if we adopt the trustful attitude inherent in Jesus' final prayer. To trust God with what we can't change is to accept it as unchangeable and leave the results—including the "why?"—to God.

WHEN IT'S EASY

For some, placing what they can't change in God's hands may come simply and easily—once *they recognize the need* for it. It did for forty-five-year-old Jill (from chap. 1) who was so resistant to aging. Jill dyed her hair, dressed youthfully, watched her weight, and exercised rigorously to look young. Nevertheless, ageism comments still bothered her, particularly jokes about older people. One distasteful joke about an old woman could put her in a bad mood for a week. One day as Jill thought about this while bike riding, it occurred to her that she had another option: she could accept her age and learn to live with it. "Father," she prayed, "aging is a part of your design. I accept it and I give you my concerns about it."

To verify her acceptance, she rode to the youth director's office. She said to Tom, "I have a confession to make. I can't help you with chaperoning any more because I'm not under forty. I'm forty-five, soon to be forty-six."

Tom looked embarrassed. He said, "I'm sorry I made that announcement about chaperones having to be under forty. Groping for words to attract people with a youthful attitude, I said the wrong thing. I've regretted it ever since. We want you for a chaperone, and we need you."

WHEN IT'S DIFFICULT

For most of us, a one-time prayer like Jill prayed will not be enough to deposit our circumstances into God's hands. We may not have her trusting nature. Our situation may be so difficult that we look at hers and say, "What's aging compared to my problem?"

Jesus' prayer was one of genuine trust in God. It was not a prayer of resignation, "Okay, God, you win." Arriving at trust like Jesus exhibited will not come effortlessly. For some of us, it may be as difficult as praying for God to forgive those who have wronged us (chap. 14). There's no quick fix, but there are some prayer exercises we can do to aid the process.

We may need to start with our lack of trust. If we have been truly shocked by what happened to us, or if it seemed out of line with our concept of God, we may find ourselves reluctant to trust him. Or, our pain may be so bad we question whether God cares. We may have to begin the depositing process by acknowledging our lack of trust: "Father, I've been deeply hurt by what happened. I want to trust you again, but I am afraid to. I give you my fear so that I can eventually give you what I can't change."

To develop trust, we may need to pray Jesus' prayer over and over, making it a part of our regular prayers. A woman whose husband was mentally ill writes, "My experience has been that acceptance comes as a daily decision, much like setting the thermostat in the living room. It is a verbal affirmation before the Lord, 'Even though I do not understand what's happening, I do love and trust you, even now.' "[5]

Just as Jesus used the words of a psalmist, we may need to use someone else's words. We could paraphrase Jesus' prayer: "I have done all I can do. My efforts are exhausted. I give, I relinquish, the situation to you. With childlike trust I deposit my situation in your hands." Or, we could adapt E. Stanley Jones's prayer: "I am yours and this thing concerns me, and so this is yours, too. I surrender it to you."[6]

We may need to do something that signifies the fact that we have given our situation to God. Imagine what you can't change as a burden you are holding in your hand, much the same way you would hold a basketball or a bowl of fruit. As you talk to God about the burden, as you "see" it before you, sense its heaviness. When you have told him all about it, hand the burden to him (extend your hands upward). As you hand it to him, say, "Here I give it to you. I cannot carry it any longer."

Similarly, you might want to write about your burden on a piece of paper. Afterwards, burn the paper or tear it up in tiny pieces and release it to the wind: "I trust my burden to you; it is no longer a part of me."

Or, hold a grain of wheat in your hand. Visualize it as the seed of what you can't change. Bury it in the ground, symbolizing the burial of your resistance to accepting your situation. Watch for it to grow (John 12:24). As you watch, affirm what God is going to do in your life: "Father, I have died to the life I have. I am looking forward to the new life you have for me."

Break down what you can't change into smaller chunks and give one chunk at a time to God. Often what we can't change has many facets to it. If we can analyze it so that we can see the various facets, then we can give one facet at a time to God.

A PICTURE OF TRUST

In their book *Trusting God Again,* Glandion Carney and William Long tell the story of a boy by the name of Ron who had AIDS. Visiting this eleven-year-old in the hospital, Carney tried to explain to him what it means to trust God. Taking off his wedding ring, he opened his shirt pocket and dropped it in. Then he said, "Trust is like that, Ron. It's like taking the thing that is dearest to you and dropping it right into your heart, just like a farmer would drop a seed into the ground. Then, as it touches your heart, it becomes warm and begins to grow. Trust is like that—to take the most precious thing that you have and drop it right into your heart. God is then the one who nurtures it and makes it warm and makes it grow."[7]

In a way, what we can't change is a precious thing. We hold on to it as if it were a valuable treasure we need to protect and to preserve. As long as we hold on, peace will elude us. We must open our clenched fists that clutch our treasure before our hands can be free to hold something else. Once we accept what we cannot change, then we can use our time and our energy to focus on what we can change and what we can do.

WHAT WE CAN DO

A hospice doctor encouraged Edmund to accept his inevitable death. While Edmund believed in a life after death, it was the loss of the "now" that bothered him. The doctor helped him to see that the "now" still had potential. The doctor said, "Your muscles are atrophying, but you still have your mind, and you still have your verbal abilities. Use them. Record your history of what you are going through, what you are thinking and feeling, as this disease progresses. This history can be used to help others who suffer from the same disease."

When our focus shifts from what we have lost to what we have, from what we can't change to what we can, then we know we have accepted our situation. The inner wrestling is replaced by inner peace. The agitation ceases. Calmness returns to our spirit as we are freed of the internal strife that continually robbed us of inner harmony. Not everyone's *unchangeable* can have a glorious ending, but they can all have a peaceful ending.

MAKING YOUR WILL MINE

What will I need to relinquish to experience peace and serenity?

How will accepting what I cannot change enable me to see what I can change?

What are some ways I can deposit what I cannot change into God's hands?

"In thee, O Lord, do I put my trust. . . . Into thine hand I commit my spirit."[8]

CHAPTER 17

RELEASE FROM THE VISE

*No matter what happens to us, we hold in our
hearts the joy of the Lord, submerged at times by
pain or adversity, but always deep within our
beings. We may indeed suffer, but He was
crucified and yet rose again. No matter what
happens to us we know that beyond the Cross lies
the Resurrection.[1]*

EMILY GARDINER NEAL

When I asked Russ (from chap. 1) what was the most
difficult part of dealing with Sara's accident and injuries, he
said, "The feeling of helplessness. There is no way I can
change what has happened, and there is no way I can fix
the physical scars Sara has suffered."[2]

This feeling of helplessness is what makes "being in a
vise" an apt description of what we can't change. Caught in
its jaws, we feel like there's nothing we can do, but that just
isn't true. We can pray like Jesus prayed.

LESSONS FROM JESUS' PRAYER LIFE

We can take the various lessons we have learned from studying Jesus' prayer life and apply them to our own situations.

1. *We can visit lonely places.* We can imitate Jesus' deliberate withdrawals to be alone with God. In solitude, God can refresh us, strengthen us, and guide us. We can align our will with God's will so we may stay on track as believers.

2. *We can express gratitude as Jesus did.* We can do so during bright shining moments and during the difficult times too. Allan (from chap. 1) discovered this after his wife Ruth died. "In every thing give thanks: for this is the will of God in Christ Jesus concerning you" (1 Thess. 5:18) became embedded in his mind. Allan said, "I couldn't seem to shake it or replace it with anything else. I had not been reading in 1 Thessalonians at the time, but it seemed that this was the message the Lord had for me."[3] Indeed it was, because it enabled Allan to cope. He counted himself a fortunate man as he appreciated the kind of woman Ruth was, the number of years they were married, and the two fine daughters they had raised. He said, "God couldn't have given me a more appropriate word."[4]

3. *We can honestly express our emotions.* In Jesus' praying, there was no pretense, no cover-up, no repression of feeling. In front of a group of people, as he headed toward Jerusalem and the cross, he said, "Now is my soul troubled" (John 12:27). Deeply distressed and full of anguish, Jesus said, "My soul is overwhelmed with sorrow" (Mark 14:34; Matt. 26:38, NIV) when he prayed for an escape from the cross. On the cross, Jesus cried, "My God, my God, why hast thou forsaken me?" (Mark 15:34). Honest praying gave

God a channel for ministering to his needs, and it will do the same for us.

4. *We can adopt Jesus' attitude of trust and confidence by giving God what we can't change.* Through any number of prayer exercises, we can deposit what we can't change into God's hands the way a gardener buries a seed. Putting the seed into the ground implies a willingness to let go. Covering it with dirt says, "I'm taking my hands off and leaving it to you." Standing up, patting the dirt with our foot, and looking at the horizon says, "I can't wait to see what this grain will eventually produce" (cf. Hab. 2:1a).

5. *We can rely on Jesus' intercession.* As we walked with Jesus from his baptism to the cross, we learned how much effort he put into his prayer life. Praying about what we can't change is not simple or easy. As Allan related, "If ever there was a time in my life that I didn't feel like giving thanks, it was after Ruth's death. I had just been deprived of the companionship of the one person who meant more to me than life itself, and being thankful was hardly what I was experiencing."[5]

If we are honest, we may be just as skeptical as Allan was about praying Jesus' way. Or, we may become too exhausted to pray. Our faith may weaken, or we may be in too much pain to concentrate. Our fears may overwhelm us. At those times, we can be comforted by knowing that Jesus is praying. His loving intercession will not forget us. What Jesus did for Peter and for his disciples, he does for us in his perpetual role as intercessor.

6. *We can count on God to answer us.* Even though many of the answers Jesus received to his prayers didn't spell *End of Struggle,* God always answered Jesus.

* When Jesus wanted to know if his disciples were beginning to grasp who he was, Jesus prayed. In

response, God gave him Peter's confession, "You are the Christ" (Matt. 16:16, NIV).

* When Jesus realized his time was limited and he needed to choose men to train to carry on his ministry, he spent the night praying. When morning came, he called his disciples to him and chose twelve of them to be apostles (Luke 6:12–13).

* When the disciples didn't understand the nature of Jesus' ministry and when Jesus himself needed confirmation, God responded with the transfiguration experience.

* After Jesus prayed, "Now is my soul troubled," God gave him strength to go on to Jerusalem toward the cross.

* After his plea for escape in the garden of Gethsemane, God strengthened Jesus in such a way that he calmly proceeded toward the cross. Throughout the arrest and his trials, Jesus—more than Pilate, more than those who sought his arrest—appeared to be in control.

* After his cry of abandonment from the cross, fellowship between the Father and the Son was restored. Jesus died with a shout of triumph on his lips (John 19:30) and with the confidence of a child falling asleep in his father's arms.

We can trust God to respond in the same way to us. His answers will be sufficient.

RESULTING BENEFITS

What most of us were looking for when we decided to walk with Jesus from his baptism to the cross was the ability to cope with what we can't change. Our only thought might have been, *If I can just get through this,* and that is what praying Jesus' way will do for us. It will enable us to cope, yet it does more than that. The seed that dies "produces many grains" (John 12:24, TEV).

* *Release from the vise.* When we pattern our prayer life after Jesus', the vise will release its grip over us. All along we felt like the grip was outside of us, as if there were actually a physical vise holding us against our will. Yet when we deposit what we can't change into God's hands, then we discover that the vise was on the inside where it affected our outlook and held our energy hostage.

Released from its grip, we feel free—and we are. We are no longer in bondage to what we can't change.

* *Inner peace.* Jesus said, "Take my yoke upon you and learn from me" (Matt. 11:29a, NIV). When we identify with Jesus and learn from him, we, in return, receive rest for our souls (Matt. 11:29b). The anxiety over what we can't change ceases.

* *Perspective change.* To understand the illness of depression, I began studying it. What I learned about depression was so insightful that I wrote a book on understanding a woman's depression. When a psychiatrist's secretary read it, she said, "You are right on target. You know women, and you know the subject of depression."

Pleased with her comments, I started singing along with the car radio as I drove home. While singing, I mused over what Bob and I had been through. In my musing, I thought I heard the words, "God meant it for my good."

I shook my head, trying to clear my mind.

The words came again: "God meant it for my good."

I turned off the radio, and in the quiet I heard the words again: "God meant it for my good."

Hadn't Joseph said something similar to that after he

reconciled with his brothers who sold him into slavery (Gen. 50:20)? When I checked the reference, a window in my soul opened. I could see better, and I felt a lightness in my spirit. The depression no longer seemed like an awful black pit; rather, it seemed to be a passage leading to a new life, and indeed it has been that.

* *Personal growth.* In researching depression, I learned about the power the subconscious can have over the conscious. I learned what it means to be a woman, and that knowledge helped me begin to live in harmony with myself. I learned I had faulty thinking patterns, like ruminating and overgeneralizing. What I learned was so life changing that I would hate to think what my life would be like today if I hadn't changed. While I would never want to be depressed again, I have to admit it was one of the best things that ever happened to me.

Peggy, from chapter 1, concurs: "I can truthfully say scleroderma is the worst thing and the best thing that has ever happened to me. It is the worst because it is a devastating illness. It is the best because it made me run to my Lord with my arms empty but open wide. He has lovingly helped me look at my life and my death, my gifts and my limitations, my hopes and my fears, and most importantly, He's taught me to keep my focus on Him and Him alone. . . . I wouldn't turn down the gift of physical healing in the future, but I also wouldn't give up one thing He has taught me through having to deal with scleroderma."[6]

Every grief and disappointment we have is an opportunity for us to learn some new truth, to open some new door to a larger life, to discover new dimensions of wholeness and meaning and joy and love.

* *Growing closer to Christ.* The best part, though, for me was coming to know Jesus better. When I took hold of his

hand and began walking with him toward the cross, I identified with him. We were—and are—in life's struggle together. I began to see him as someone to learn from. His example in prayer became indelibly printed on my mind; I've used the lessons over and over again. In the "fellowship of his sufferings," my life became intertwined with his.

Others have experienced this too. In commenting about popular Christian writer Jamie Buckingham's struggle with cancer, Michael Thompson writes, "He knew Him through suffering in ways he never could before. He touched Him at levels only dreamed of when he raced from event to event in his colorful life."[7]

* *Being fully alive.* With some things that we can't change, it would be easy to begin to see ourselves as a victim and grow resentful and bitter. On the other hand, when we work through our emotions and deposit what we can't change into God's hands, we become intensely alive to the present and hopeful about the future.

As Gerald Sittser adjusted to the deaths of his wife, his mother, and his daughter, he wrote, "I was struck by how wonderful ordinary life is. Simply being alive became holy to me. As I saw myself typing exams, chatting with a student on the way to class, or tucking one of my children into bed, I sensed I was beholding something sacred."[8]

THE LIGHT OF THE RESURRECTION

While Jesus' prayers must always be interpreted in light of the cross, the cross must always be interpreted in light of the resurrection. Jesus did not stay on the cross. Release from his long struggle came in the form of the resurrection, giving purpose and meaning to all he had been through.

If we follow Jesus' way of praying, release will come for

us too. There will come a resurrection in our lives—a moment when we are free from the vise and are ready to say, "I am ready to embrace life again."

MAKING YOUR WILL MINE

Of the many lessons from Jesus' prayer life, which one was the most insightful to me?

What benefits can I expect to experience when I pattern my prayer life after Jesus'?

What changes when I accept what I cannot change?

"O Joy that seekest me through pain,
I cannot close my heart to thee;
I trace the rainbow thro' the rain."[9]

Endnotes

Chapter 1

1. William Barclay, *The Revelation of John,* vol. 2, *The Daily Study Bible* (Edinburgh, Scotland: The Saint Andrew Press, 1965), 32.
2. Russ Weiss, letter to author, 30 December 1995.
3. Ibid.
4. Peggy Brooks, letter to author, 5 November 1994.
5. Ibid.
6. Ibid.
7. From the old hymn, "O Love That Wilt Not Let Me Go," words by George Matheson, 1842–1906.

Chapter 2

1. John Claypool, *Glad Reunion* (Waco, Tex.: Word Books, 1985), 135.
2. Rebecca Manley Pippert, *Hope Has Its Reasons* (New York: Harper & Row, 1989), 191.
3. Ibid.
4. Ibid., 192.
5. Ibid., 192–93.
6. Ibid., 193.

7. Ray Summers, *Commentary on Luke* (Waco, Tex.: Word Books, 1972), 43.

8. Ibid., 44.

9. Elton Trueblood, *The Lord's Prayers* (New York, Evanston, and London: Harper and Row, 1965), 34.

10. H. I. Hester, *The Heart of the New Testament* (Nashville, Tenn.: Broadman Press, 1950, 1963), 110.

11. Leon Morris, *The Gospel According to St. Luke,* vol. 3 of *Tyndale New Testament Commentaries* (Grand Rapids, Mich.: William B. Eerdmans Publishing Company, 1974), 99.

12. William Barclay, *The Mind of Jesus* (New York: Harper and Row, 1960, 1961), 29–30.

13. Ibid., 30.

14. Trueblood, *The Lord's Prayers,* 34.

15. Herbert Lockyer, *All the Prayers of the Bible* (Grand Rapids, Mich.: Zondervan Publishing House, 1959), 181.

16. Pippert, *Hope Has Its Reasons,* 192.

17. Ibid., 193.

18. Theologian Reinhold Niebuhr's Serenity Prayer, Martin E. P. Seligman, Ph.D., *What You Can Change and What You Can't* (New York: Alfred A. Knopf, 1994), page vii. It is called "The Serenity Prayer" (1934), and is also attributed to Friedrich Oetinger (1702–1782).

CHAPTER 3

1. Trueblood, *The Lord's Prayers,* 17.

2. William L. Hendricks, *Who Is Jesus Christ?,* vol. 2 of *Layman's Library of Christian Doctrine* (Nashville, Tenn.: Broadman Press, 1985), 37.

3. *The Interpreter's Bible,* vol. 8 (Nashville, Tenn.: Abingdon Press, 1955), 85.

4. Hendricks, *Who Is Jesus Christ?,* 37.

5. William Barclay, *The Gospel of Matthew,* vol. 1, *The Daily Study Bible* (Edinburgh, Scotland: The Saint Andrew Press, 1965), 62.

6. Ibid., 63–64.

7. Kenneth S. Wuest, *First Peter in the Greek New Testament, Wuest's Word Studies* (Grand Rapids, Mich.: William B. Eerdmans Publishing Company, 1942), 67.

8. Philip Yancey, *Where Is God When It Hurts?* (Grand Rapids, Mich.: Zondervan Publishing House, 1977), 118–19.

9. Ibid., 119.

10. Ibid.

11. H. S. Vigeveno, *Jesus the Revolutionary* (Glendale, Calif.: Regal Books, 1966), 101.

12. Ibid., pages 101–02.

13. Mark 9:24b.

CHAPTER 4

1. Ronald Dunn, *When Heaven Is Silent* (Nashville, Tenn.: Thomas Nelson Publishers, 1994), 131.

2. William Barclay, *Philippians, Colossians, and Thessalonians, The Daily Study Bible* (Edinburgh, Scotland: The Saint Andrew Press, 1960), 79.

3. In this book, we are using A. T. Robertson's *A Harmony of the Gospels for Students of the Life of Christ* (New York: Harper and Brothers Publishers, 1950) to determine the chronology of Jesus' prayers.

4. Curtis C. Mitchell, *Praying Jesus' Way* (Old Tappan, N.J.: Fleming H. Revell, 1977), 18.

5. Ibid., page 18.

6. B. H. Carroll, *Messages on Prayer,* comp. J. W. Crowder, ed. J. B. Cranfill (Nashville, Tenn.: Broadman Press, 1942), 31.

7. Mitchell, *Praying Jesus' Way,* 18.

8. Psalm 5:3, NIV.

CHAPTER 5

1. Donald Zochert, *Laura: The Life of Laura Ingalls Wilder* (Chicago, Ill.: Contemporary Books, Inc., 1976), 225–26.

2. Summers, *Commentary on Luke,* 64.

3. Mitchell, *Praying Jesus' Way,* 19.
4. Gerald L. Sittser, *A Grace Disguised* (Grand Rapids, Mich.: Zondervan Publishing House, 1996), 34.
5. Ibid., 35.
6. Peggy Brooks, letter to author, 24 September 1994.
7. David Hazard, "Listening in Silence," *Charisma,* July 1996, 63.
8. William Barclay, *The Gospel of Mark, The Daily Study Bible* (Edinburgh, Scotland: The Saint Andrew Press, 1964), 131.
9. *The Interpreter's Bible,* vol. 8, 104.
10. Sittser, *A Grace Disguised,* 35.
11. Ibid., 34.
12. From the old hymn "Open My Eyes that I May See," words by Clara H. Scott, 1841–97.

CHAPTER 6

1. Sittser, *A Grace Disguised,* 37.
2. Hester, *Heart of the New Testament,* 142.
3. Ibid.
4. Ibid., 143.
5. Mitchell, *Praying Jesus' Way,* 20.
6. Ibid.
7. Summers, *Commentary on Luke,* 72.
8. *The Interpreter's Bible,* vol. 8, 113–14.
9. Acts 9:6.

CHAPTER 7

1. Barclay, *The Revelation of John,* 127.
2. Gertrude Crampton, *Tootle* (Racine, Wisc.: Western Publishing Co., Inc., 1945).
3. Barclay, *The Gospel of Mark,* 157.
4. Craig S. Keener, *The IVP Bible Background Commentary New Testament* (Downers Grove, Ill.: InterVarsity Press, 1993), 279.
5. Mitchell, *Praying Jesus' Way,* 22.
6. *The Interpreter's Bible,* vol. 7 (Nashville, Tenn.: Abingdon Press, 1955), 433.

7. Joachim Jeremias, *The Prayers of Jesus* (Philadelphia, Penn.: Fortress Press, 1967), 73.
8. Robert E. Coleman, *The Mind of the Master* (Old Tappan, N.J.: Fleming H. Revell Company, 1977), 39.
9. From the old hymn, "I'll Live for Him," words by Ralph E. Hudson, 1843–1901.

CHAPTER 8

1. Harry Emerson Fosdick, *The Meaning of Prayer* (New York: Association Press, 1915), 130.
2. Barclay, *The Mind of Jesus,* 167.
3. Ibid., 175.
4. Fosdick, *The Meaning of Prayer,* 130–31.
5. Hebrews 13:20–21, New Century Version, pronoun "you" changed to "me" by author for this prayer.

CHAPTER 9

1. Carroll, *Messages on Prayer,* 41.
2. J. W. Shepard, *The Christ of the Gospels: An Exegetical Study* (Grand Rapids, Mich.: William B. Eerdmans Publishing Company, 1956), 308.
3. John 3:14; John 6:51; Matt. 9:15; John 2:19, Matt. 16:4.
4. Implied in Luke 9:31.
5. Mitchell, *Praying Jesus' Way,* 23.
6. Summers, *Commentary on Luke,* 114.
7. *The Interpreter's Bible,* vol. 7, 458.
8. Shepard, *The Christ of the Gospels,* page 315.
9. Barclay, *The Mind of Jesus,* 180–81.
10. Ibid., 181.
11. Shepard, *The Christ of the Gospels,* 317.
12. Summers, *Commentary on Luke,* 116.
13. Carroll, *Messages on Prayer,* 40.
14. *The Interpreter's Bible,* vol. 8, 174.
15. The collect for Lent 4, *The Alternative Service Book 1980* (Hodder and Stoughton, 1980), 517, cited in Margaret Mag-

dalen, *Jesus, Man of Prayer* (Downers Grove, Ill.: InterVarsity Press, 1987), 131.

CHAPTER 10

1. John P. Newport, *The Lion and the Lamb* (Nashville, Tenn.: Broadman Press, 1986), 173.
2. Morris, *The Gospel According to St. Luke,* 121.
3. Hab. 3:18a, NIV; Matt. 11:26b.

CHAPTER 11

1. The sequence of the selected scenes is based on A. T. Robertson's *Harmony of the Gospels for Students of the Life of Christ.* The dialogue in the scenes is not verbatim from the Bible; rather, it is the author's version of what could have been said based on the biblical accounts.
2. Mitchell, *Praying Jesus' Way,* 30.
3. *Luke–John, The Broadman Bible Commentary,* vol. 9 (Nashville, Tenn.: Broadman Press, 1970), 322.
4. You may verify this disagreement by noting where the punctuation marks are in different Bible versions of John 12:27–28a.
5. Author's paraphrase.
6. Psalm 25:17.

CHAPTER 12

1. Stuart Sacks, *Hebrews Through A Hebrew's Eyes* (Baltimore, Md.: Lederer Messianic Publishers, 1995), 1–2.
2. Margaret Magdalen, *Jesus, Man of Prayer* (Downers Grove, Ill.: InterVarsity Press, 1987), 113.
3. James G. S. S. Thomson, *The Praying Christ* (Grand Rapids, Mich.: William B. Eerdmans Publishing Company, 1959), 119.
4. Ibid.
5. Christians differ on the rightness or wrongness of praying to Jesus and to the Holy Spirit. For a discussion on this topic, see

chapter 8 of Brenda Poinsett, *Prayerfully Yours* (Nashville, Tenn.: Broadman Press, 1979).

6. Carroll, *Messages on Prayer,* 52.
7. Ibid.
8. Psalm 110:4b.
9. From the old hymn, "Hail, Thou Once Despised Jesus," words by John Bakewell, 1721–1819.

CHAPTER 13

1. Paul Thigpen, "Losing and Finding My Father," *Charisma and Christian Life,* June 1990. Used by permission.
2. Magdalen, *Jesus, Man of Prayer,* 122.
3. Ibid., 121.
4. Mitchell, *Praying Jesus' Way,* 59.
5. Ibid., 59.
6. Ibid., 60.
7. Ibid., 61.
8. Ibid., 62–63.
9. Ibid., 64.
10. Dunn, *When Heaven Is Silent,* 131.
11. John M. Koessler, "Keys to a Healthy Emotional Life," *Decision,* September 1991, 27.
12. Ibid., 27.
13. Karen Burton Mains, *Karen! Karen!* (Wheaton, Ill.: Tyndale House Publishers, Inc., 1979), 54.
14. This idea of growth and gain when facing death baffled me until I read *Dying Well: The Prospect for Growth at the End of Life* by Dr. Ira Byock (New York: Riverhead Books, 1997). I find the concept both challenging and liberating.
15. Mark 14:36, TEV.

CHAPTER 14

1. Mary Grunte, coauthor of *How to Forgive When You Don't Know How,* quoted by Dianne Hales in "Three Little Words That Will Heal You," *McCall's,* June 1994, 104.
2. Acts 7:60, NIV.

CHAPTER 15

1. Magdalen, *Jesus, Man of Prayer,* 142.
2. Mitchell, *Praying Jesus' Way,* 70.
3. Barclay, *The Gospel of Matthew,* 406–07.
4. Trueblood, *The Lord's Prayers,* 121–22.
5. Ibid., 122.
6. J. Grant Swank Jr., "Reaching into the Night," *Decision,* March 1992, 29–30.
7. Ibid., 30.
8. Ibid.
9. Ibid.
10. Ibid.
11. Ibid.
12. Ibid.
13. Ibid.
14. Randal Earl Denny, *In the Shadow of the Cross* (Kansas City, Mo.: Beacon Hill Press of Kansas City, 1995), 111.
15. Ibid.
16. Ibid.
17. General Articles on *Matthew–Mark, The Broadman Bible Commentary,* vol. 8 (Nashville, Tenn.: Broadman Press, 1969), 246.
18. Psalm 69:1–3a, TEV.

CHAPTER 16

1. Bob Buford, *Halftime* (Grand Rapids, Mich.: Zondervan Publishing House, 1994), 56.
2. Author's paraphrase.
3. William Barclay, *The Gospel of Luke, The Daily Study Bible,* (Edinburgh, Scotland: The Saint Andrew Press, 1964), 301–02.
4. William Barclay, *The Gospel of John,* vol. 2, *The Daily Study Bible* (Edinburgh, Scotland: The Saint Andrew Press, 1964), 301.
5. Helen Grace Lescheid, "The Place of Acceptance," *Discipleship Journal* 60 (1990): 17.

6. E. Stanley Jones, *Victory Through Surrender* (Nashville, Tenn.: Abingdon Press, 1966), 110.

7. Glandion Carney and William Long, *Trusting God Again* (Downers Grove, Ill.: InterVarsity Press, 1995), 20.

8. Psalm 31:1a, 5a.

CHAPTER 17

1. Emily Gardiner Neal, *The Healing Power of Christ* (Carmel, N.Y.: Guideposts Associates, Inc., 1972), xii.

2. Russ Weiss, letter to author, 31 March 1996.

3. Allan Poage, letter to author, 21 December 1994.

4. Allan Poage, letter to author, December 1993.

5. Poage, 1994 letter.

6. Peggy Brooks, letter to author, 11 August 1994.

7. Michael Thompson, "A Different Perspective," *The Trumpet* 26, no. 3 (March 1992): 2.

8. Sittser, *A Grace Disguised,* 36–37.

9. From the old hymn, "O Love That Wilt Not Let Me Go," words by George Matheson, 1842–1906.

BIBLIOGRAPHY

Barclay, William. *The Gospel of John,* Vol. 2, *The Daily Study Bible.* Edinburgh, Scotland: The Saint Andrew Press, 3d ed., 1964.

Barclay, William. *The Gospel of Luke, The Daily Study Bible.* Edinburgh, Scotland: The Saint Andrew Press, 3d ed., 1964.

Barclay, William. *The Gospel of Mark, The Daily Study Bible.* Edinburgh, Scotland: The Saint Andrew Press, Seventh Impression, 1964.

Barclay, William. *The Gospel of Matthew, The Daily Study Bible.* Edinburgh, Scotland: The Saint Andrew Press, Sixth Impression, 1965.

Barclay, William. *Philippians Colossians, and Thessalonians, The Daily Study Bible.* Edinburgh, Scotland: The Saint Andrew Press, 2d ed., 1960.

Barclay, William. *The Mind of Jesus.* New York: Harper and Row, 1960, 1961.

Carney, Glandion, and William Long. *Trusting God Again: Regaining Hope After Disappointment or Loss.* Downers Grove, Illinois: InterVarsity Press, 1995.

Carroll, B. H. *Messages on Prayer,* J. W. Crowder, comp., J. B. Cranfill, ed. Nashville, Tennessee: Broadman Press, 1942.

Coleman, Robert E. *The Mind of the Master*. Old Tappan, New Jersey: Fleming H. Revell Company, 1977.

Corbishley, Thomas. *The Prayer of Jesus*. Garden City, New York: Doubleday & Company, Inc., 1977.

Denny, Randal Earl. *In the Shadow of the Cross*. Kansas City, Missouri: Beacon Hill Press of Kansas City, 1995.

Dunn, Ronald. *When Heaven Is Silent*. Nashville, Tennessee: Thomas Nelson Publishers, 1994.

Fosdick, Harry Emerson. *The Meaning of Prayer*. New York: Association Press, 1915.

Hazard, David. "Listening in Silence," *Charisma*, July 1996, 63.

Hendricks, William L. *Who is Jesus Christ? Layman's Library of Christian Doctrine*. Nashville, Tennessee: Broadman Press, 1985.

Hester, H. I. *The Heart of the New Testament*. Nashville, Tennessee: Broadman Press, 1950, 1963.

Jeremias, Joachim. *The Prayers of Jesus*. Philadelphia, Pennsylvania: Fortress Press, 1967.

Jones, E. Stanley. *Victory Through Surrender*. Nashville, Tennessee: Abingdon Press, 1966.

Keener, Craig S. *The IVP Bible Background Commentary New Testament*. Downers Grove, Illinois: InterVarsity Press, 1993.

Koessler, John M. "Keys to a Healthy Emotional Life," *Decision*, September 1991, 27-28.

Lescheid, Helen Grace. "The Place of Acceptance," *Discipleship Journal*, 60. (1990): 16-19.

Lockyer, Herbert. *All the Prayers of the Bible*. Grand Rapids, Michigan: Zondervan Publishing House, 1959.

Mains, Karen Burton. *Karen! Karen!* Wheaton, Illinois: Tyndale House Publishers, 1979.

Magdalen, Margaret. *Jesus, Man of Prayer*. Downers Grove, Illinois: InterVarsity Press, 1987.

Mitchell, Curtis C. *Praying Jesus' Way*. Old Tappan, New Jersey: Fleming H. Revell, 1977.

Morris, Leon. *The Gospel According to St. Luke*, Vol. 3, *Tyndale New Testament Commentaries*. Grand Rapids, Michigan: William B. Eerdmans Publishing Company, 1974.

Pippert, Rebecca Manley. *Hope Has Its Reasons*. New York: Harper & Row, 1989.

Poinsett, Brenda. *When Jesus Prayed*. Nashville, Tennessee: Broadman Press, 1981.

Poinsett, Brenda. *Prayerfully Yours*. Nashville, Tennessee: Broadman Press, 1979.

Robertson, A. T. *A Harmony of The Gospels for Students of The Life of Christ*. New York and London: Harper and Brothers Publishers, 1950.

Sacks, Stuart. *Hebrews Through A Hebrew's Eyes*. Baltimore, Maryland: Lederer Messianic Publishers, 1995.

Shepard, J. W., *The Christ of the Gospels: An Exegetical Study*. Grand Rapids, Michigan: William B. Eerdmans Publishing Company, 1956.

Sittser, Gerald L. *A Grace Disguised*. Grand Rapids, Michigan: Zondervan Publishing House, 1996.

Summers, Ray. *Commentary on Luke*. Waco, Texas: Word Books, 1972.

Swank, Jr., J. Grant. "Reaching Into The Night," *Decision*, March 1992, 29-30.

The Broadman Bible Commentary. General Articles, *Matthew-Mark*, Vol. 8. Nashville, Tennessee: Broadman Press, 1969.

The Broadman Bible Commentary. Luke–John, Vol. 9. Nashville, Tennessee: Broadman Press, 1969.

The Interpreter's Bible, Vol. 7. Nashville, Tennessee: Abingdon Press, 1955.

The Interpreter's Bible, Vol. 8. Nashville, Tennessee: Abingdon Press, 1955.

Thomson, James G. S. S. *The Praying Christ*. Grand Rapids, Michigan: William B. Eerdmans Publishing Company, 1959.

Trueblood, Elton. *The Lord's Prayers*. New York, Evanston and London: Harper and Row, 1965.

Vigeveno, H. S. *Jesus the Revolutionary*. Glendale, California: Regal Books, 1966.

Wuest, Kenneth S. *First Peter in the Greek New Testament, Wuest's Word Studies*. Grand Rapids, Michigan: Wm. B. Eerdmans Publishing Company, 1942.

Yancey, Philip. *Where Is God When It Hurts*. Grand Rapids, Michigan: Zondervan Publishing House, 1977.